The Literacy Kit

Inform, Explain, Describe

Geoff Barton

OXFORD

OXFORD

UNIVERSITY PRESS

Great Clarendon Street, Oxford OX2 6DP

Oxford University Press is a department of the University of Oxford.

It furthers the University's objective of excellence in research, scholarship, and education by publishing worldwide in

Oxford New York

Athens Auckland Bangkok Bogotá Buenos Aires

Cape Town Chennai Dar es Salaam Delhi Florence Hong Kong Istanbul

Karachi Kolkata Kuala Lumpur Madrid Melbourne Mexico City Mumbai

Nairobi Paris São Paulo Shanghai Singapore Taipei Tokyo Toronto Warsaw

with associated companies in Berlin Ibadan

Oxford is a registered trade mark of Oxford University Press
in the UK and in certain other countries

© Geoff Barton 2001

First published 2001

The moral rights of the authors have been asserted

Database right Oxford University Press (maker)

ACKNOWLEDGEMENTS

Crown Copyright material, extract from leaflet: 'Mobile Phones and Health' (Department of Health), is reproduced under Class Licence Number C01P0000148 with the permission of the Controller of HMSO and the Queen's Printer for Scotland.

We are also grateful to the following for permission to reprint copyright material:

Atlantic Syndication for article by Bill Mouland and Stephen Wright: 'An Ealing Comedy of Errors', *Daily Mail*, 8.11.00

BBC for extract on 'Mobile Phones' from Newsround website, 20.7.00 and extract from Science Shack website, 28.3.01

David Higham Associates for extract from Michael Asher: *A Desert Dies* (Viking, 1986) and extract from James Herriot: *It Shouldn't Happen to a Vet* (Michael Joseph, 1972)

Hodder and Stoughton Ltd for extract from Keith Waterhouse: *City Lights* (1994)

Hodder and Stoughton Educational Ltd for extract from *Young Citizen's Passport* (The Citizenship Foundation 2000)

The Independent for article by Ian Herbert: 'In a Lancashire village, a cat a day is vanishing into thin air. What is going on?', *The Independent*, 20.11.99

News International Syndication for article by Jamie Pyatt: 'Flying Solo', *The Sun*, 10.11.00 and for interview with Des'ree by Danny Danzinger 'Best of Times/ Worst of Times', *The Sunday Times Magazine*, 11.3.00

Oxford University Press for adapted extract from Abigail and Philip Buckle: *Graphic Products to GCSE* (OUP, 1997)

Private Eye Magazine (Pressdram Ltd) for 'The Glamis Herald', *Private Eye*, 8.4.94

Radio Times for article: 'My Kind of Day', Millvina Dean, Survivor of the Titanic, talking to David Gillard, *Radio Times*, 23 December 2000-5 January 2001

J Sainsbury plc for leaflet: 'An Easy Guide to Healthy Eating – The Vegetarian Way'

Abner Stein for extract from Steve Callahan: *Adrift* (Bantam, 1986)

Times Educational Supplement for extracts from article by Pamela Coleman, TES 25.8.00

Transworld Publishers for extracts from Bill Bryson: *Down Under* (Doubleday, a division of Transworld Publishers, 2000), copyright © Bill Bryson 2000

The Vegetarian Society for extract 'Animals and the environment' from their website (www.vegsoc.org)

We have tried to trace and contact all copyright holders before publication. If notified the publishers will be pleased to rectify any errors or omissions at the earliest opportunity.

We are grateful to the following for permission to reproduce photographs:
Corbis/Mark Mason studios (cover); Ace Photo Agency, pp9, 116; Adams Picture Library, pp26, 47, 96, 102, 106; Ardea Wildlife & Pets, p63; Camera Press, p118; Capital Pictures, p19 (top); Eye Ubiquitous, p21; Hutchison Library, p52; Mary Evans Picture Library, pp40, 41, 78; Oxford Scientific Films, p55; PA Photos, p92; Photostage/Donald Cooper, pp133, 136; Robert Harding Picture Library, p35; Ronald Grant Archive, p17; Science Photo Library, pp81, 85, 107, 125; Topham/Picturepoint, pp13, 90; Universal Pictorial Press, pp18, 19 (bottom), 39, 60, 66; John Walmsley, p4
Other photographs by Alex Hibbs

The cartoon illustrations are by David Semple.

A CIP catalogue record for this book is available from the British Library.

ISBN 0 19 832038 8

Printed in Spain by Graficas Estella SA.

Orders and enquiries to Customer Services:

Tel: 01536 741068 **Fax:** 01536 454519

Contents

Introduction

Inform, Explain, Describe is a central part of *The Literacy Kit*. It provides the core texts you will need for developing pupils' reading, writing and spoken work.

You may have used one of the starter activities in the **Lesson Starters** boxes to kick the lesson off, and **OHTs** from the relevant pack to initiate whole-class discussion of text types. Now comes the developmental stage, in which students focus on the specific word-, sentence- and text-level objectives of the *Framework for Teaching English 11–14*.

This Students' Book provides you with texts that are closely mapped to all the objectives and organized on a year-by-year basis, enabling you to plan more carefully and to ensure that essential text types are covered in each year. The **Objectives** box at the head of each text extract details the objectives addressed.

The texts always begin with an **Introduction**. This is a brisk, context-setting starter which tunes pupils into the type of text they are looking at. It will get them focusing on the language features and issues they can expect to be dealing with. You may want to develop this, asking pupils to make predictions before they start to read the text.

The **texts** themselves have been carefully selected to highlight some key features of structure and language, and to match the appropriate levels of interest and ability of pupils in different year groups. You'll find plenty of texts on contemporary subjects that should appeal to boys and girls aged 11–14.

The questions which follow provide for two levels of response. **Understanding the text** asks straightforward, fact-spotting questions. Don't underestimate the importance of these: they are the questions that quickly build pupils' confidence in skimming and scanning, helping them to identify key points quickly.

Interpreting the text offers more open-ended questions. Here pupils will need to give more reflective responses, often writing short paragraphs explaining and justifying their thoughts.

The **Language and structure** section highlights the new emphasis on language skills within the Framework. These are not arid, 'spot the split infinitive' style questions. Their focus is on language in use, getting pupils looking at writers' language decisions, cataloguing features of the text and then commenting on effect. This is the central part of the literacy process – emphasizing effect, and not simply spotting language features.

The **Writing activity** focuses on an aspect of the text and gets pupils responding in writing in a more developed way. They may be asked to practise a language skill in greater detail, or to rewrite part of the text in a different style. Importantly, this is the part of the process that shifts the emphasis from reading to writing. Having explored features of the writer's approach in a text, pupils now begin to write for themselves. It is part of the process of scaffolding writing.

Each unit concludes with an **Extended writing** task. Here the emphasis on developing pupils' writing skills is consolidated. These are bigger, more ambitious tasks which link back to the texts that pupils have been exploring. The tasks are scaffolded with suggestions, hints and, often, starter sentences. This approach should help pupils in the transition from dependent to independent writers.

Speaking and listening is integral to all English work and we know that you will be talking to students about their perceptions of texts throughout the process. We have also built in specific speaking and listening tasks where they develop language skills, or provide an opportunity to meet one of the *Framework* objectives.

In the **Teacher's Book** you will find a wealth of related resources, and the **OHT** pack provides those all-important acetates for a shared, whole-class focus on texts.

The Literacy Kit is, as you can see, a completely integrated scheme. I've been using it with my students here in Suffolk and the response to the variety, the rapid pace, and the sheer range of materials has been terrific – even from my more reluctant pupils!

I hope it proves similarly enjoyable and useful for you, helping you with the planning and delivery of the *Framework* in a lively and systematic way. Most of all, I hope your students have fun with the huge variety of new resources here.

Your feedback, via the website, would be very welcome.

Geoff Barton
www.oup.com/uk/litkit

What are information texts?

Purpose and audience

Information texts need to be clear and easy to understand. Their audience might know nothing about a topic and want to learn (for example, 'A Beginner's Guide to Playing the Guitar'); or they may already know something about the topic but need more detail (for example, 'The Advanced Guide to Website Design').

Text level features

Information texts often contain complex information and must present it as clearly as possible. This may mean using a range of **layout features**. You might expect to find:

- headings and subheadings
- short paragraphs
- different font styles, bold and italic print
- bullet points
- diagrams.

The sequence of information will be important. The text may start with **general statements**, followed by more **detail** later. **Examples** will often be included.

Sentence level features

Information texts are often written in the **present tense** ('Diet is an important concern …'). They may use an impersonal style, with the **third person** ('Diet is …') rather than first or second person ('I think …' or 'You should …').

Information texts will often use **connectives** to help the reader follow the organization of ideas – for example, *then, so, next.*

Word level features

Information texts may use **technical terms** and complex language if appropriate. Generally these texts will use vocabulary which gives facts rather than a lot of description.

Formal writing

Young Citizen's Passport

> ### OBJECTIVES
>
> With this extract we examine a text that gives information in an organized way. These are the objectives you will be studying:
>
> - Word level: *connectives*
>
> - Sentence level: *tense management*
>
> - Reading: *evaluate sources, identify main ideas, media audiences* (how texts are tailored to their audience), *print, sound and image,* and *non-fiction style* (how writers match language and organization to their intentions)
>
> - Writing: *organize texts appropriately,* and *present information*
>
> - Speaking and listening: *recall main points*

Introduction

This text is aimed at young people and aims to inform them about their rights and responsibilities. Explore the way it presents the information. When you have studied this text, you will have a chance to write an information text of your own. If possible, start by reading the questions in Section A, then listen to the text being read aloud. This will help you to listen for clues about how the text has been organized.

young citizen's **passport**

Part-time work

At what age?

The law controlling the work of young people below school leaving age varies from one town or country to another. Under the *Children and Young Persons Act 1933,* each local authority creates its own by-laws giving the terms and conditions for the employment of young people in that area.

Employment rights

In 1994, senior judges decided that UK laws unfairly discriminated against part-time workers. As a result, many of the rights of those in part-time jobs (even if it's for only a couple of hours per week) are the same as those of people in full-time employment.

These state the kind of work that a young person may, or may not, do and require employers to inform the council of all young people they employ. Although largely ignored, the rules also state that, generally speaking, anyone below school leaving age who has a part-time job must have a medical certificate of fitness for work and an employment card issued by the local council.

The only kind of employment children under fourteen can be given is occasional light farm work, supervised by a parent, or parts in plays or films, etc., for which a special licence is required from the local authority.

Children aged fourteen or over may be employed only in light work approved by their local authority.

No young person below school leaving age may be employed before 7am or after 7pm, for more than one hour before the start of school, or for more than two hours on a school day, or on a Sunday.

New rules require a magistrates' licence for someone between 14–16 to be paid to take part in sport.

There are few restrictions on the employment of 16 or 17 year olds. However, people under 18 cannot normally work in a bar, unless they work in a restaurant where drinks are served with meals, or are being trained for the licensing trade under a Modern Apprenticeship scheme. Copies of the by-laws controlling the employment of young people in your area can be obtained from the local library, council or education office. Information is also available from the Low Pay Unit.

A boy of 14, working in a factory making beds, suffered severe injuries when his arm was trapped in an unguarded machine. A court fined his employer £1000 for failing to fit a guard to the machine and £200 for employing a child. The employer also paid £438 towards the cost of the case.

young citizen's **passport**

UNDERSTANDING THE TEXT

1 What kind of work may children under the age of 14 legally do?

2 Is the age for starting work the same in all areas?

3 How long may a child under 16 work before the start of the school day?

4 In what kind of bar may people under 18 work?

INTERPRETING THE TEXT

5 An information text for young people should look lively and attractive. Look at the layout of the page. How has the designer tried to do this here? Say something about:

- ◆ the images
- ◆ the use of boxes and panels around text
- ◆ the choice of font styles.

6 Look at the first paragraph – what is the source of the facts about what the law says? How much can you 'trust' in what you have learnt from this text? Does giving the source make the text feel reliable and factual? Write a brief paragraph explaining your response.

LANGUAGE AND STRUCTURE

1 Information texts can be written in the third person, like this:

No young person below school leaving age may be employed …

They can also be written in the second person, like this:

If you are below school leaving age, you may not be employed …

Choose one paragraph and rewrite it using the second-person form. Does this make it sound more personal? Write a sentence saying whether you think the text becomes more or less easy to follow as a result.

2 Information texts are usually written in the present tense. Find an example in this text of a sentence in the past tense. Say why this change of tense is necessary.

3 Information texts need to be clearly organized. How are different points linked together in this text? Write down three words or phrases which the writer uses to link ideas.

> ## HINT
> - Linking words and phrases might include:
>   *These, that, another, also, secondly, next*

4 The writer of an information text often makes some general points and then backs them up with specific examples.

Use a table like this to show two examples of the way this writer supports ideas with examples. Fill in the missing information.

General point	Supporting example(s)
Only certain kinds of work are available for children under 14	
	People under 18 cannot normally work in a bar

WRITING ACTIVITY

Imagine you are working for a student advice service and you receive a letter asking for advice:

I am thirteen and I wish to get a part-time job. I have been offered a paper round by my local newsagent. Am I allowed to take it and, if so, what hours am I allowed to work?

Duncan

Write a short information text for Duncan. It should cover the rules for employing young people which are relevant to his case. Remind yourself of the features of information texts, such as using the third person and the present tense. Your text should be clearly organized and give examples. Then write a brief letter to Duncan, explaining that you are enclosing this information sheet.

Informal writing

A Guide to Health

Introduction

This information text was created by Nick Vollmer, a Year 9 student, in his PSE lessons. His class had been studying ways of staying healthy. His homework was to design a leaflet informing other students about eating healthily. When you have read his work, you will have the chance to present the information in a different way.

UNDERSTANDING THE TEXT

1 What are the four main types of foods?

2 Write down one tip that the writer gives for creating a balanced diet.

3 How much food does the average person eat in a lifetime?

4 What are micronutrients?

Nick Vollmer of W2

A GUIDE TO HEALTH

The Statistics

How much should we be eating?

- 25-30% of the food we eat should be FATS
- 15-20% of the food we eat should be PROTEIN
- 55-60% should be CARBOHYDRATE

Fun Facts

- ☺ In you're lifetime, you eat 100 tonnes of food
- ☺ Macronutrients means fats, protein, and carbohydrates
- ☺ Mircronutrients means vitimins & minerals

All Health

- ☢ You can be physically or mentally unhealthy
- ☢ Physically unhealthy is when you are e.i. over weight or on drugs
- ☢ To be mentally unhealthy is when e.i. you're stressed

Types of Food

This will help you to under stand what catagories foods come under

- Carbohydrates- Any foods containing wheat
- Dairy- Any foods or drink containing milk or butter
- Meat, fish, protein- Meats, fish, or foods containing protein
- Fruit & Veggies- apples, oranges, potatoes, etc.

A balanced Diet

- ✔ You should get 5-9 servings of carbs. a day
- ✔ 5-9 servings of friut and veggies a day
- ✔ Try to get 2-3 servings of dairy foods a day
- ✔ When you eat meat, fish, or protein, try to keep it in a low fat regoin. But try to get 2-3 servings a day
- ✔ Use fatty, sugary foods sparingly

Note: Use a variety of foods!!

INTERPRETING THE TEXT

5 If you had to pick out the three main ideas in the text, what would they be?

6 Information needs to be presented clearly. Nick Vollmer uses some diagrams (e.g. the pyramid) and some images (e.g. clip-art showing a pig on a bike). Which of his presentational devices do you think work best? Which would you have done differently?

7 The leaflet is aimed at students aged 11–14. How might the text have been different if it was aimed at:

    a an older audience (e.g. aged 35–50)

    b a younger audience (9–11)?

LANGUAGE AND STRUCTURE

1 Look at the way the writer organizes his information. Compare the information he puts on each side of his leaflet by completing these sentences:

    a The first side of the leaflet gives information on …

    b The second side of the leaflet gives information on …

2 The writer uses a variety of sentence functions in the leaflet. Find an example of:

    ♦ a statement

    ♦ a question

    ♦ a command.

3 Nick Vollmer is writing for an audience aged 11–14. A good information text will use language to appeal to its age group. Find examples where Nick:

    ♦ uses headings to grab the reader's interest

    ♦ addresses the reader directly.

4 Information texts can include commands that directly address the reader. Look at the tone this writer uses when he gives commands. He could have said: 'Eat 2–3 servings of dairy foods a day'. This would sound impersonal and more like an order. How does he make his commands seem more personal and friendly?

5 Nick Vollmer's leaflet contains a number of spelling or typing errors. He uses a personal spelling notebook at school. Which words do you notice that he should add to his book and learn to spell accurately?

6 Imagine you are Nick Vollmer's teacher and you are marking his leaflet. What feedback would you give him? What do you think are its strengths and weaknesses?

Writing as if you are his teacher, give him three brief comments on:

a the presentation of the leaflet

b the way he uses language

c suggestions of ways to improve it.

You could also give him a grade or mark out of ten.

WRITING ACTIVITY

For some audiences you might want a leaflet to have a more formal, impersonal tone. You might want to emphasize the facts more, rather than the personal advice to the reader.

On one side of A4, use the information from Nick Vollmer's leaflet and present it in a more formal, impersonal way.

Try to:

♦ avoid addressing the reader directly

♦ avoid compressing words (e.g. say 'it is' rather than 'it's')

♦ avoid any comic or chatty details.

Quickly put together your leaflet. What kind of audience do you think it would be best suited to?

EXTENDED WRITING

Very quickly, write down a list of points on one of the topics below. Don't try to organize them at all – just get down as many points as you can think of.

Topics

- ◆ The way your school buildings are organized (information for a visitor)
- ◆ A singer, group, or hobby that you know a lot about
- ◆ A place you have visited (e.g. on holiday or a school trip).

As a homework activity, you could do some research on one of the topics so that you have more factual information.

Once you have gathered the information, create a short information text – for example, 'A Visitor's Guide to this School' or 'Essential Facts about Majorca'.

Working on your own, create an information text which:

- ◆ uses the present tense
- ◆ has an impersonal, factual tone
- ◆ organizes the information you have collected in a way that is useful to the reader.

Then make up five factual questions about your information.

Read your information text to a partner, then ask her or him to answer the questions. See how far he or she has followed the main points of your text. Ask for feedback about whether you could have made any of it clearer, and if so, how.

What are recounts?

Purpose and audience

Recounts are texts which tell us about events. They may be designed to inform us (such as, in a history textbook, a description of the build-up to a battle); or they may be more personal – a diary entry or autobiography describing an event in a person's life.

The audience may already be familiar with the topic or writer, or the information may all be new. The writer will usually structure his or her ideas in **chronological order** – that is, the events will be retold in the sequence in which they happened.

Text level features

Because they are usually chronological, most recounts will begin with an **opening paragraph** describing the setting or the start of the event; the **last paragraph** will usually be about the end of the event or its aftermath. Paragraphs in between will use **connectives** to link the sequence of ideas together.

Sentence level features

Recounts may use the **first person** (for stories and autobiography) or **third person** (for factual reports). They will usually use the **past tense**. There may be a variety of **sentence types** to hold the reader's interest. Short sentences may be used to build tension or suspense. Sometimes a writer may use **dialogue** to move the story forward or tell us more about a character.

Word level features

Recounts often aim to answer the questions: *who, what, when, where, why?* Writers paint pictures with words, so we may find descriptive writing, with techniques such as **similes** and **metaphors** used to create vivid images. Writers' choice of words may include the simple or complex, the formal or informal, depending on what they are aiming to achieve.

Autobiographical writing
Millvina Dean, Survivor of the Titanic

OBJECTIVES

With this extract, we will focus on the features of a personal recount, written informally. You will study these objectives:

- Word level: *connectives*

- Sentence level: *tense management*, *sentence variety*, and *vary formality*

- Reading: *evaluate sources*, *identify main ideas*, *infer and deduce* (understand implied meanings from evidence in the text), and *language choices* (how they enhance meanings)

- Writing: *drafting process* (planning and writing), *organize texts appropriately*, *present information*, and *evocative description*

Introduction

When the Titanic sank in 1912, more than 1500 lives were lost. Nowadays, few of the survivors of the disaster are still alive. But here is one, Millvina Dean, thinking back (in a *Radio Times* article) about her life. When you have studied her recount, you can try writing one of your own.

Millvina Dean, Survivor of the Titanic

I can't bear ice in my drinks – it always makes me think of the iceberg, you see. I'm the youngest *Titanic* survivor – there are only five of us left – as I was nine weeks old when it sank in 1912, so obviously I can't remember anything about it. But my poor father drowned that day and whenever I imagine an iceberg I think of him. His body was never found – it may still be in the ship. I'm 88 and, latterly, the *Titanic* has totally changed my life.

Until a few years ago I was living quietly in retirement in the New Forest, but now much of my time is spent travelling all over the world to speak at conventions as a guest of the various *Titanic* societies. I'm an honorary member of eight – in Canada, America, two in Ireland, Scotland, France, Germany and here in England. Until the wreck was discovered there wasn't nearly so much interest in the disaster. My mother, who died in 1975, didn't tell me about what we'd been through until I was eight. She'd be absolutely amazed that I've become a sort of celebrity because of it.

My whole family – my father Bertram, my mother

Georgetta and my 18-month-old brother, Bertram Vere – was on that maiden voyage. We were going to start a wonderful new life in America – my father planned to open a tobacconist's shop in Kansas City. We travelled steerage – that's third class – and most of the third-class passengers were to die because they couldn't get from the lower decks to the lifeboats. I'm convinced that my father was a hero and that his quick response saved us. My mother was woken by a loud crash, and Father immediately told her to go to the lifeboats with the children. He kissed her goodbye and said he would see her later – but she never saw him again. I was bundled in a sack by a sailor and thrown into lifeboat 13. My mother followed but my little brother got separated from us and put in another lifeboat. We were all picked up by the *Carpathia*, but my dear father went down with the *Titanic*.

My mother, brother and I came back to Southampton, and I've spent all my life around the New Forest. I worked as a cartographer and a secretary and, once, as an assistant in a tobacconist's – I felt that Father would have approved. But I'd hardly given any thought to the *Titanic* when, in 1988, I was invited to attend a convention in Boston, and since then I haven't stopped. I've been to so many places that I would never otherwise have gone

to, and wherever I go people make a terrific fuss of me, which I like! And I don't mind travelling by boat – I've been on several cruises and even given a talk on the *QE2*.

I'm just back from attending the opening of an exhibition of *Titanic* artefacts in Stockholm, and now I'm off to Ireland for the opening of a restaurant named after the ship. I'm an honorary citizen of Regina, in Canada, and Kansas City, and I've been given a civic reception in Cobh in Ireland, where the *Titanic* docked before setting off for America. The local council here have even named a road after me – Millvina Close. And there are always dozens of letters from all over the world to answer. People just address them to Millvina Dean, *Titanic* survivor, Southampton – but they all arrive.

I'll be staying at home this Christmas, but I'd rather not watch the *Titanic* film. When panic sets in at the end I would be wondering about my father, and it would be too upsetting. But I have been invited to meet Kate Winslet and the director, James Cameron, and I've seen two Leonardo DiCaprio lookalikes at conventions. They were exactly like him. Very handsome.

Millvina Dean was talking to David Gillard

UNDERSTANDING THE TEXT

1 How many Titanic survivors were left at the time Millvina Dean gave her interview?

2 How old was she when the ship sank?

3 How many members of her family were on the Titanic and how many survived?

4 How is Millvina Dean still involved with the Titanic?

5 Why does she not wish to watch the film *Titanic*?

6 Summarize what you think are the three main points made in the text.

INTERPRETING THE TEXT

7 How reliable do you find Millvina Dean's account? Does her recount feel like a historical document, full of accurate facts? Say why or why not.

8 Write down one thing you learn about Millvina Dean's character from the text.

9 What is Millvina Dean's attitude to the celebrity status (fame) she has achieved? Do you think she welcomes the attention or does she try to avoid it? Write a short paragraph saying how you can tell.

> ## HINT
>
> ● Look for a sentence where she says how she feels about people making 'a terrific fuss' of her.

LANGUAGE AND STRUCTURE

1 Look at the first sentence of the article.

   a Why do you think the writer chose this as the first sentence?

   b Do you think it is a good beginning for the article?

2 Look at the end of the first sentence, where the writer uses the phrase 'you see'. Does this phrase make the text seem …

more chatty – more formal – more informal – too relaxed – friendly – like a letter

Choose the best description. Then write a sentence explaining your choice.

3 Recounts can use a wide range of sentences. Most of Millvina Dean's sentences are complex, e.g. 'We travelled steerage – that's third class – and most of the third-class passengers were to die because they couldn't get from the lower decks to the lifeboats.'

A few sentences are simple, e.g. 'They were exactly like him.'

Which of these statements do you think best describes the effect of this range of sentences? Choose the opening of the statement you most agree with, and then finish it off in your own words.

a The variety of sentences makes the text vivid because …

b The variety of sentences makes the text hard to follow because …

c The variety of sentences holds our interest because …

d The variety of sentences makes the text feel like a spoken account because …

4 How does the writer link the different ideas in the text together? Look for three words or phrases which help to do this.

5 Recounts are usually written in the past tense. Here, the writer describes the events of the Titanic using the past tense, and writes about her life now using the present tense. Find sentences which illustrate both tenses.

Past tense:

Present tense:

6 Although Millvina Dean's recount is not all in chronological order, some paragraphs *do* tell events in the order they happened. Which paragraphs do this?

7 At the end of the text it says 'Millvina Dean was talking to David Gillard'. In other words, the article is based on an interview. Yet it is written as if it were a personal account. Does this change your view on how valid or reliable the text is?

Write a sentence or two describing how you think the text has been written, and by whom.

8 Using the article you have read, complete this fact file about Millvina Dean:

Name:

Age:

Where she lives:

What she now does:

What she did earlier in her life:

What happened to her father:

What happened to her mother, her brother and herself on the Titanic:

How the Titanic disaster has affected her life positively and negatively:

What kind of person she is:

WRITING ACTIVITY

Take the facts from Millvina Dean's article, which you gathered for question 8 above. Think about a different way that they might be presented. Imagine you were writing an article about Millvina Dean for a local newspaper. Your focus is what happened on the Titanic, rather than her thoughts and feelings now. Your aim is to communicate to readers the panic and fear of the night the Titanic sank, and the way one survivor got free.

Aim to:

- write in the past tense
- structure the article chronologically (i.e. in the order it happened)
- use connectives (*then, next, after that, later*) to link paragraphs together
- use an impersonal style (avoid saying 'I' or 'me').

Write the first 150 words of your article. Use a headline like this:

The Night the Titanic Sank: Memories of a Survivor

Use a topic sentence for the opening paragraph (a sentence which summarizes the whole story – *who, when, where?*).

Finally, write a brief paragraph comparing your version with Millvina Dean's article.

- How different are they?
- How might they appeal to different audiences?
- What problems did you encounter in your rewriting?

Personal recounts

My First Day at School

Introduction

This section contains four short texts in which different people describe their first day at school. The extracts were first published in a newspaper article called 'My First Day at School'. Use them to develop your note-taking skills, and to explore the way writers use structure and details to bring their recounts alive. When you have finished, you will have a chance to write your own recount.

My First Day at School

The traumas and joys of starting school, as told to **Pamela Coleman**.

ESTHER RANTZEN, Chairman, ChildLine

I was two-and-three-quarters when I started school and it was a traumatic time. I did not want to go and on the first day sat very gloomily on the steps outside the house. My mother took me. I didn't scream and kick, I was just terribly miserable.

I know everybody is hugely in favour of pre-school play groups and nursery schools, but I remember thinking that making things out of egg boxes was pointless. I sent my own children to nursery school at three-and-a-half and I think that is a better age to start.

For the first three or four weeks at school I painted nothing but black pictures, which reflected how I felt at the time, and it was regarded as quite a breakthrough when I put my first dab of colour on the paper. Later on, however, I was one of those children who was very happy at school.

GLENYS KINNOCK, MEP for South Wales East

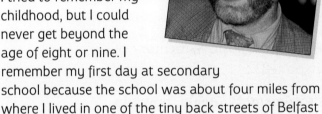

My grandmother lived next door to the national school in Holyhead in Anglesey, and on my first day I went to her house to have a cup of tea before joining my brother who was already in the juniors. I wasn't nervous about starting school.

The reception class teacher, Miss Morgan Jones, was very large and very cuddly and very nice. This was in 1949 and there weren't a lot of sweets about and my eyes immediately fell on a big Kilner jar of dolly mixtures, which was sitting on the mantelpiece. There was a fire in the grate and the milk crate was on the hearth to keep the little bottles of milk warm and the room felt very welcoming. There was also a rocking horse and one of those tubular steel rockers in which two children sat, one at each end.

At the end of the day you got a sweetie if you'd been good, and most children were good in Miss Morgan Jones's eyes.

BRIAN KEENAN
Novelist and former Beirut hostage

When I was held hostage I tried to remember my childhood, but I could never get beyond the age of eight or nine. I remember my first day at secondary school because the school was about four miles from where I lived in one of the tiny back streets of Belfast and I took a bus to get there. It was the first time I'd travelled on a bus without my parents.

All the lads in the street who were also starting at the school were with me and although I knew their faces, I was aware there was something different about them. What was different, I suddenly realized, was that we were all wearing school uniforms.

Everyone was apprehensive about starting a new school and there was an incessant din on the bus of boys talking and shouting. The school colours were orange and black – the badge on the jacket, the turn-down tops of the socks, the tie, the piping along the grey v-neck sweater you had to wear – and that and the noise of the scene reminded me of the swarm of bees or wasps.

BENJAMIN ZEPHANIAH
Poet

My twin sister, Velda, and I started school together at St Matthias primary in Hockley, Birmingham, which doesn't exist any more. When the time came for Mum to leave us with the teacher, Velda started crying and she wouldn't stop. Eventually she was moved to another room because she was causing such a disturbance.

I thought school was fun. I remember making a little building with building blocks and being surprised that all we did was play, because Mum had said you went to school to learn.

Velda and I were the only two black kids in the school, which frightened me a bit. After a while, when we could still hear Velda crying in the distance in some far corner of the school, the children asked me if she was my sister and I totally disowned her.

It's really weird the way things ended up: she really liked school later on and I hated it. She did well and I was the one who rebelled and got expelled.

UNDERSTANDING THE TEXT

1 Make a set of notes which show clearly:

◆ the name of each speaker

◆ what the speaker is best known for

◆ two or three main points of what they remember about the first day at school.

> **HINTS**
>
> ● Organize your notes clearly on the page – leave lots of space
>
> ● Use bullet-points to keep points brief (remember that you don't need to use full sentences for bullet-points)
>
> ● Use underlining to add emphasis to the names of the people

2 Glenys Kinnock has vivid memories of a teacher. Summarize the information we learn about this teacher.

INTERPRETING THE TEXT

3 Which speaker do you think has the most positive memory of the first day at school? How can you tell?

4 Which speaker has the least positive memory? Again, how can you tell?

5 Which speaker's experience of school sounds most different from the kind of school you first attended? Think about activities you did at school and the teachers you have known. Do they remind you of the experiences described by the writers? Write a brief paragraph to explain your answer.

LANGUAGE AND STRUCTURE

1 Recounts are usually divided into paragraphs about different parts of the subject. They may use complex sentences with subordinate clauses, where information is packed together densely.

Choose either the Glenys Kinnock or the Benjamin Zephaniah text. Then:

a write a very brief summary of what each paragraph is about (ideally try to use just one word – e.g. 'teacher', 'classroom', 'sister')

b write a sentence saying why the paragraphs are in this order – would they make sense in a different one?

c choose one paragraph and say how its opening sentence helps prepare the reader for some new information

d choose a complex sentence and say whether it is easy to follow or not.

2 Choose either the Esther Rantzen or the Brian Keenan text and look at whether the writer uses the past tense, present tense or both. Write down which it is, then give a reason why the writer may have used tenses in this way.

WRITING ACTIVITY

Think back to a teacher who made an impact on you. It might be someone in primary school or more recently. Think about:

◆ how the teacher looked

◆ the classroom he or she taught you in

◆ his or her personality and teaching style

◆ why the teacher made such an impression on you.

In pairs, talk about the teachers you remember. Using the bullet-points above, ask questions about your partner's teacher. You might be asked to report back to the class on this teacher.

Next, write a three-paragraph summary of your memories of your own teacher. Use the same format as the texts in this unit.

Remember to:

◆ use the first person

◆ use the past tense

◆ use vivid details to bring the memory to life

◆ link paragraphs together with connectives.

EXTENDED WRITING

Earlier in this unit you wrote a description of a teacher who had made an impression on you. Now think back to your memories of first going to school. What can you remember of:

♦ the school

♦ your first classroom

♦ your first teacher?

Write a recount which tells readers about your memory of the first day.

Aim to:

♦ use the past tense

♦ structure your ideas chronologically

♦ use connectives to link ideas together

♦ use a personal tone (e.g. 'I … me')

♦ use detail to help the reader visualize the scene.

Your main aim should be to entertain your reader. Try to bring the memory to life as vividly as you can.

What are explanation texts?

Purpose and audience

Explanation texts aim to help us understand the world. They may explain how something works, or why things are the way they are. They are often aimed at readers who have a particular interest in the topic, or who know a little and wish to know more. It is therefore essential that these texts are very clearly written and presented.

Text level features

The layout of these texts is often designed to help them get their explanations across to the reader. This might mean the use of **question and answer** formats, or **short paragraphs**, **bullet-points** and **checklists**. Ideas may be structured in a **step-by-step** way, so that readers build their understanding logically. The steps may even be **numbered** to make the sequence clear.

Sentence level features

These texts will usually be written in the **present tense** – explaining how things are now (except where they are explaining an event from history). They might use the **active voice** (e.g. 'The scientist then places the magnesium in the dish …') or the **passive voice**, where the person doing the action is less important than what is done (e.g. 'The magnesium is then placed in the dish …'). The last part of the text might be a **summary**.

Word level features

The writer might include **specialist language**, depending on a) the topic and b) the audience. A glossary may be included to help explain any technical terms. The writing will usually be **direct** and **impersonal**, with little description, so that the essential facts are as clear as possible.

Formal and informal writing
Mobile Phones

OBJECTIVES

This section presents two texts for you to compare. They both aim to explain the same type of information. These are the objectives you will be studying:

- Word level: *connectives*

- Sentence level: *starting paragraphs, paragraph structure, sequencing paragraphs,* and *vary formality*

- Reading: *compare presentation, evaluate sources, identify main ideas, media audiences* (how texts are tailored to their audience), and *non-fiction style* (how writers match language and organization to their intentions)

- Writing: *drafting process* (planning and writing), *organize texts appropriately,* and *develop logic*

Introduction

In this unit you can compare two texts. Both aim to explain a similar topic – the risks to young people of using mobile phones. Text A is a leaflet produced by the Department for Health. Text B is a page from the Newsround website, aimed at a young audience.

Compare the way the two texts explain the information. When you have finished, you can write an explanation text of your own.

Text A

Mobile phones and health: Children and young people under 16

Mobile phones are very popular with young people and have obvious attractions for personal security and keeping in touch with others. Parents and young people should make their own informed choices about the use of mobile phones. The current balance of evidence does not show health problems caused by using mobile phones. However the research does show that using mobile phones affects brain activity. There are also significant gaps in our scientific knowledge. Because the head and nervous system are still developing into the teenage years, the expert group considered that if there are any unrecognised health risks from mobile phone use, then children and young people might be more vulnerable than adults.

The expert group has therefore recommended that in line with a precautionary approach, the widespread use of mobile phones by children (under the age of 16) should be discouraged for non-essential calls.

In the light of this recommendation the UK Chief Medical Officers strongly advise that where children and young people do use mobile phones, they should be encouraged to:

- use mobile phones for essential purposes only
- keep all calls short – talking for long periods prolongs exposure and should be discouraged.

The UK CMOs recommend that if parents want to avoid their children being subject to any possible risk that might be identified in the future, the way to do so is to exercise their choice not to let their children use mobile phones.

Text B

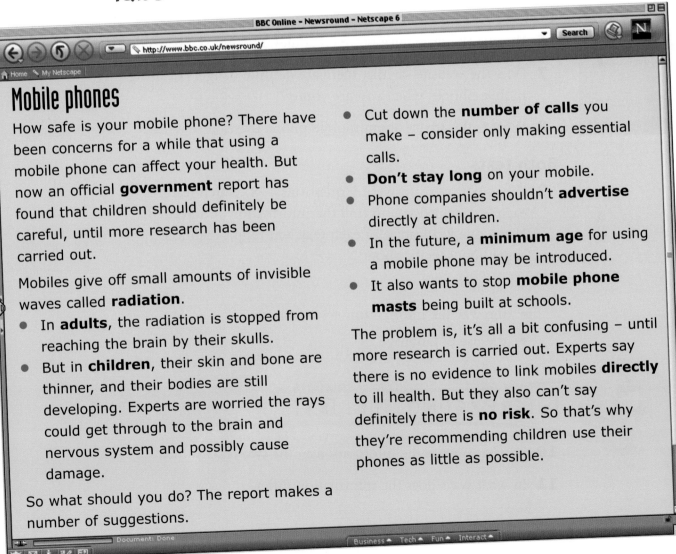

BBC Online – Newsround – Netscape 6

http://www.bbc.co.uk/newsround/

Mobile phones

How safe is your mobile phone? There have been concerns for a while that using a mobile phone can affect your health. But now an official **government** report has found that children should definitely be careful, until more research has been carried out.

Mobiles give off small amounts of invisible waves called **radiation**.

- In **adults**, the radiation is stopped from reaching the brain by their skulls.
- But in **children**, their skin and bone are thinner, and their bodies are still developing. Experts are worried the rays could get through to the brain and nervous system and possibly cause damage.

So what should you do? The report makes a number of suggestions.

- Cut down the **number of calls** you make – consider only making essential calls.
- **Don't stay long** on your mobile.
- Phone companies shouldn't **advertise** directly at children.
- In the future, a **minimum age** for using a mobile phone may be introduced.
- It also wants to stop **mobile phone masts** being built at schools.

The problem is, it's all a bit confusing – until more research is carried out. Experts say there is no evidence to link mobiles **directly** to ill health. But they also can't say definitely there is **no risk**. So that's why they're recommending children use their phones as little as possible.

UNDERSTANDING THE TEXT

Text A

1 What two reasons does the leaflet give for young people using mobile phones?

2 Does it state that mobile phones carry a health risk?

3 What are the findings of the expert group?

4 What are UK CMOs?

5 What advice does the leaflet give young people about using mobile phones?

Text B

6 What is the difference between adult and child skulls?

7 Does the website say that there are definite dangers in using mobile phones when you are young?

8 What is the advice about mobile phone masts at schools?

Both texts

9 When you were answering questions 1–8, which features of each text helped you to find the information you needed? Name one key feature of each text. You might mention something specific about:

♦ layout

♦ the way the information is structured

♦ the use of language.

INTERPRETING THE TEXT

10 In what ways is the information in the two texts similar?

11 In what ways does the information differ?

12 An explanation text should be carefully structured. Look more closely at the way these texts organize their information. How do the two writers structure their texts to make their explanations clear? You might look at:

♦ how the information is introduced at the beginning

♦ the sources that are given for the information

♦ how ideas are linked together by connectives

♦ layout features that help to present information.

LANGUAGE AND STRUCTURE

1 Look carefully at the two texts. Try to find a sentence from each text which states the same basic message. Write down these two sentences. Is there anything you notice about differences between the two sentences, such as:

♦ length

♦ complexity

♦ the kind of vocabulary the writer uses?

2 a What clues are there in the layout and structure that Text A is aimed at an older audience?

b How can you tell from the layout *and language* that Text B is aimed at a younger audience?

> ### Hints
>
> Look for any differences in:
>
> ● the way the texts are organized
>
> ● different types and lengths of sentences
>
> ● different choices of words.

3 Looking more closely at Text B, can you say how you think information on websites is often presented differently?

4 Explanation texts sometimes include questions. The writer of Text B does this at the beginning of paragraphs one and three. What is the purpose of these questions?

5 Look at this statement:

Text A uses scientific language and is more formal. Text B is less scientific and more informal.

Do you agree or disagree? Write down your answer giving an example from each text to support it.

WRITING ACTIVITY

Explanation texts aim to place their ideas in the order which will best help the reader to follow them. This means that sentences are often linked by connectives such as *because, next, another,* or *so.* These words show how one sentence links to the next.

Take the list of facts on the next page. The sentences are presented in the wrong order. If you were using this information to create a fact sheet about Elizabeth the First, which order would you use? How would you link ideas using connectives? Present the information as a piece of continuous text for young readers.

Think about:

◆ How you will organize this information – dividing it into general points and examples.

◆ How you will link the ideas together using connectives like *so* and *although.*

1 She was Queen of England from 1558–1603.

2 Elizabeth I was born in 1533.

3 She died in 1603.

4 At this time, England was in conflict with Spain.

5 Elizabeth I resisted getting married.

6 This was a period when explorers from Europe were sailing to discover new parts of the world.

7 New lands were claimed and new foodstuffs were brought back home.

8 Many people tried to arrange courtships for her.

9 The Spanish Armada was defeated by the English fleet in 1588.

10 It was a time of high adventure and excitement.

11 Courtiers included the Earl of Essex, the Earl of Leicester and Sir Walter Raleigh.

12 The war with Spain continued throughout her reign.

In pairs or groups, discuss how you approached this task and any problems you encountered.

Extended Writing

Choose a topic you have been studying in a different subject – for example, something from science, history or PSE. Imagine your English teacher knows nothing about this topic. Your job is to explain it to her or him as clearly as possible on one side of A4.

Design a website or factsheet about the topic. Remember that you are being asked to *explain* a process or an event. Your text should answer a specific question, such as 'Why do trees need sunlight?' or 'Why are cigarettes so dangerous?'.

Your teacher will then give you feedback on how clear your explanation was.

Think about:

- how you will organize your text

- how you will use layout features to make your explanation clearer

- how technical the information will be

- how formal your vocabulary and sentence types will be

- what tone you will use to address the reader.

What are instructional texts?

Purpose and audience

Instructions show the reader how to do something, usually in a sequence of steps. The level of detail in instructions will depend on how much the reader already knows. A 'Beginner's Guide to the Internet' may contain more general information than a specialist guide, such as 'Programming in HTML'.

Text level features

The **layout** will often be carefully designed to help the reader follow instructions – clarity will be essential. **Diagrams** may also be used to show how to do something. The text will be structured in a **logical order** and, to make it even clearer, points may be **numbered** in sequence. The writer might also add reassuring comments, or tips, to help the reader: 'Three quick steps to a delicious pudding ...'. 'If this seems time-consuming, don't worry – it will be worth it.'

Sentence level features

Sentences will often be **imperatives** (commands), with the verb near the beginning:

First *take an egg*. **Boil** it.

Sentences will often address the reader **directly**: 'If you need to check this . . .'. They will often be **short**, so that they are simple to follow, and will use **connectives** to link ideas together, such as *next, then, now*.

Word level features

Vocabulary will often be **plain** and straightforward, except where the intended reader is already an expert in the topic. There will be little use of adjectives, adverbs and imagery: the writer will be aiming at clear instructional writing rather than using too much descriptive detail.

Giving informal instructions
Telepathic Powers

> ### OBJECTIVES
>
> With this extract we examine a straightforward set of instructions. These are the objectives you will be studying:
>
> - Sentence level: *active or passive voices, sequencing paragraphs, vary formality,* and *speech and writing* (investigating their differences)
>
> - Reading: *locate information, active reading, identify main ideas,* and *non-fiction style* (how writers match language and organization to their intentions)
>
> - Writing: *organize texts appropriately, present information,* and *instructions and directions*
>
> - Speaking and listening: *answers, instructions, explanations,* and *oral text types* (how spoken texts are organized)

Introduction

Instructional texts often show people how to do things they don't already know. This text is from a book of magic tricks. It aims to teach a young audience how to do a trick involving 'telepathic powers'. When you have finished studying it, you can try writing your own instructions.

Before you read the text, look at the questions in *Understanding the text*.

Telepathic Powers

Effect This is an ideal trick to perform at a party where there are lots of people.

Ask one of your friends to leave the room for a few moments. While he or she is out spread a number of cards around on the floor, face up. Now ask a second friend to point to one of the cards.

Explain that you are going to ask the first friend to return to the room and then you'll point to several different cards. When you point to the card chosen by the second friend, the first friend will call out '*that's it!*'

Emphasise that you will not speak to them nor give any secret signals—it's all done by telepathy.

Method You do in fact have a secret signal. But try as they might, your friends won't be able to discover it!

When you spread the cards (about 15 or 20) on the floor you make sure there are two or three picture cards among them.

When your friend is out of the room arrange for one card to be selected by another friend. The friend outside the room is now asked to return and you point to various cards.

The secret signal is that when you point to a picture card your friend knows that the *next* card will be the one selected by someone in the room.

If a picture card has been chosen as the selected card you simply point to one of the other picture cards first. Your friend will then know that the next card will be the selected one.

Presentation Explain that you and your friend have been experimenting with telepathy and want to demonstrate your amazing powers!

Variation This trick can also be performed with the cards face down. You will need a pack of cards with multicoloured backs. If there is black amongst the colours, all you do is point to other colours until you want to cue your confederate. You then point to the

black area on the back and the next card will be the selected card.

You can also point to the top left hand corner until you cue your friend. The signal is that you point to the top right hand corner of a card and the next one is the selected card.

Understanding the Text

Before reading

1 Think about your own ability to give instructions. How clear and precise are you? If you were teaching someone to do a card trick, or to tie a school tie, how would you organize the instructions?

2 How would you change your instructions if the audience were older or younger?

3 If the audience already knew quite a bit about the topic, would that change the way you gave instructions?

4 Make some predictions about the text from the magic book. It is aimed at a young audience, probably aged between 9 and 14. How do you predict it will address the audience? Will it be chatty, friendly, formal, impersonal? Will it address the reader as 'you'? Will it refer to the writer as 'I' and 'me'?

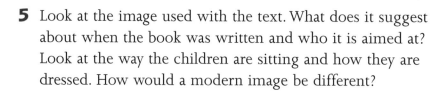

5 Look at the image used with the text. What does it suggest about when the book was written and who it is aimed at? Look at the way the children are sitting and how they are dressed. How would a modern image be different?

After reading

6 In a sentence, how does the trick work?

7 How does the 'variation' work?

8 In the picture, how can you tell who is doing the trick?

INTERPRETING THE TEXT

9 The writer has divided the text into short paragraphs, using some subheadings. How could the writer have organized the information to make the instructions even clearer?

10 Look back at the predictions you made when you answered question 4. Write a brief review (2–3 sentences) saying whether the writer's style is similar to what you predicted. For example, is the tone more or less chatty than you expected? What other differences or similarities were there?

LANGUAGE AND STRUCTURE

1 Instruction texts tend to use command sentences which begin with a verb, such as 'Ask one of your friends …'.

a Find another command sentence in this text.

b Find a sentence which is a statement rather than a command.

2 The writer's style is sometimes formal. Look more closely at this paragraph:

If a picture card has been chosen as the selected card you simply point to one of the other picture cards first. Your friend will then know that the next card will be the selected one.

The first sentence starts by using the passive voice: 'If a picture card has been chosen …'.

a How could this sentence be written in the active voice?

> **HINT**
> ● You may want to use 'If your friend …' as the beginning of the sentence.

b The final phrase 'the selected one' also sounds quite formal. Look at all of the second sentence and write it in a style which is more informal and friendly.

3 How would the instructions for this trick be different if you were *telling* a friend about the trick, rather than giving written instructions? How would you change:

◆ the overall structure

◆ the sentences

◆ the vocabulary

◆ the tone?

Would you address the audience differently?

Imagine you are speaking to a friend and telling her or him about the trick. Write down what you would say. Then write a brief paragraph describing the differences between your spoken version of the trick and the written version.

WRITING ACTIVITY

How could you use layout and language to make these instructions clearer and quicker for the reader to take in? You might use:

◆ headings, subheadings and numbers

◆ diagrams and labels

◆ bullet-points.

Produce your own version of the instructions on one side of A4, aiming for clear, simple vocabulary and sentence structures.

EXTENDED WRITING

Working in pairs, give your partner instructions on how to do an everyday task – e.g. tying a school tie, or tying up shoe laces. Give spoken instructions which your partner follows as you speak. Listen to the way you use language and how you know whether to add more information (e.g. 'no, not there – put it over the other side').

How would you give the information differently in a written text, where you could not react to the other person's actions?

Now try to write the 'Foolproof Guide' to tying a tie or shoe laces.

Write a set of instructions which you are certain will help even the most incompetent reader to get the process right.

You might:

◆ use step-by-step commands

◆ add friendly hints

◆ use diagrams and graphics to help make your instructions clearer.

Give your instructions to someone to test out. Ask for feedback. How well do your written instructions work? What could you have done to make them clearer?

What are descriptive texts?

Purpose and audience

Descriptive texts aim to give us detail. In a brochure, we might get a description of a product. Both fiction and non-fiction writers will use descriptive writing to help us to visualize people or places. The level of description used will depend on the writer's aims. A short story may contain a brief but vivid description of a character; a film review may give a detailed description of the way a film is structured.

Text level features

These texts may begin with general **opening statements** (e.g. 'I remember my own schooldays') and then move into a series of descriptive sentences which add **detail** rather than new points. Nouns and verbs will often be modified by **adjectives** and **adverbs** (e.g. 'the *reddish* bricks', 'walking *painfully*').

Sentence level features

Descriptive texts may be in the **third person**, particularly in advertising and reviews; or they may use the **first person**, especially in autobiographical writing and some stories. The **tense** will vary too. Descriptions will often be in the present tense ('Ickworth Park is glorious in the spring'), except in fiction and autobiographical writing ('The school buildings looked large and threatening'). Sentences may be longer because they will use **modification** – adjectives and adverbs – to add detail.

Word level features

Vocabulary will be **precise** and **vivid**. There may be **imagery** (such as the use of similes and metaphors) in order to help the reader to visualize what is being described. The writer may use **technical words** in some contexts (a brochure about a new car, for example). **Connectives** such as *and, also, similarly* will be used to link ideas together.

Describing a place
Memories of Leeds

Introduction

Descriptive writing takes many forms. Here the journalist Keith Waterhouse thinks back to his childhood in Leeds and describes the excitement of wandering around the maze of old shops there. When you have finished studying it, you can try writing a vivid description of your own.

GLOSSARY

Polonies – *spicy sausages*

Gastronomic – *relating to food*

Aperture – *small opening*

Clerestory – *a row of high windows, as found in churches*

Hanker after – *desire*

Board man – *an inspector from the local Schools Board*

Memories of Leeds

The Horse Meat Shop in the stew of tumbledown premises at the side of the Market was always a draw, principally because it took very little imagination to visualise the unappetising purplish joints and lumps of yellow fat in the window as horse, and partly because its frontage was painted in a vivid red, like blood; I liked to hear my mother tell me, as she often did, that it had to be painted this colour by law, to distinguish it from ordinary butchers' shops.

The herbalist's shop in Vicar Lane, with row upon row of little saucers containing powdered ginger, bee salve, prune and senna mixture, licorice root, cinnamon, dragon's blood (was it real dragon's blood?), was also good for a stare.

So was the Murder Shop whose window display of scissors and kitchen knives I imagined in my confused way to be murder weapons. There was a secondhand bookshop at the bottom of Kirkgate where I could actually finger the old books in the nothing-over-sixpence trough outside, but it was to be some years before I would dare venture inside. Back to the modern: the Polyfoto studio on Boar Lane was a much talked about recent arrival to Leeds: the latest high-speed camera snapped twenty-four pictures of you and you selected those you wanted enlarged to the postcard or cabinet size from a specimen sheet. Examples of these multi-snap sheets were in the window and I would pause to count up in how many wasted exposures the subject was blinking.

The pork shops were always an attraction, and I would feast my eyes on their marble slabs of pies and pasties and polonies, not out of hunger but simply because these gastronomic displays were visually pleasing – particularly the bisected veal, ham and egg pies in Redman's in the County Arcade, which always left me puzzling how they got a whole hard-boiled egg into the middle of a meat pie. It was while I was figuring this out one day – they would cook an ordinary oblong pie, I reasoned, then scoop out an egg-shaped quantity of meat, then wedge the egg into the aperture, then seal the pie up again with some kind of edible glue – that I thought I spotted the Board Man keeping an eye on me from across the Arcade. It was not him at all, I saw at once, just someone waiting for his wife to come out of the corset shop; but it did set me wondering how I should explain things had the Board Man been following me and seen that while I had given barely a glance to the toy shop up the Arcade with its Meccano suspension bridge in the window, here I was staring at pork pies and previous to that at the Horse Meat Shop and the Murder Shop, and then Montague Burton the Tailor of Taste (not only did I admire Burton's decorated clerestory glazing but I was beginning to hanker after a Burton's suit).

It was, as I could readily acknowledge in moments of insight, weird behaviour for a boy of eight or nine. I suppose I was a weird child all round.

UNDERSTANDING THE TEXT

1 What does Keith Waterhouse mean when he says that 'The Horse Meat Shop … was always a draw'?

2 What does he find particularly fascinating about that shop?

3 What was the Murder Shop? Why does he call it this?

4 How does his description of the herbalist's shop show that he is a child?

5 Why do you think Keith Waterhouse is anxious about the Board Man?

INTERPRETING THE TEXT

6 Which of these words best describes the way Keith Waterhouse presents himself in this extract?

curious　　*fascinated*　　*childish*　　*nervous*　　*optimistic*　　*young*

Write a sentence explaining your choice.

7 How does the shopping area described feel different from town and city centres today? You might mention:

◆ the way the shops are organized

◆ what they sell

◆ their names

◆ what they look like.

LANGUAGE AND STRUCTURE

1 One way writers can create vivid description is by using lists of details within sentences, for example:

little saucers containing powdered ginger, bee salve, prune and senna mixture, licorice root . . .

a Write down another example of this 'list' technique in the text.

b What is the effect of this way of describing things?

2 Descriptive texts may also use words describing colour and texture. Write down some examples of Keith Waterhouse's words or phrases which use the senses of sight and touch.

3 The text uses mostly long, complex sentences, with many subordinate clauses. Why do you think Keith Waterhouse uses these rather than short, simple sentences?

> ### HINTS
> ● Think about the effect short sentences would have – how would the text feel different?
> ● How do the long sentences, full of detail, help us to visualize the scene?

4 This is a personal piece of writing. In what ways does the writer use language which is personal – showing us the thoughts and feelings of a young child?

5 Writers can use imagery to bring their descriptions alive. Using your own words, write down the picture the following phrases create in your mind. The key words of each are highlighted. Does the image recall something you have seen or experienced yourself?

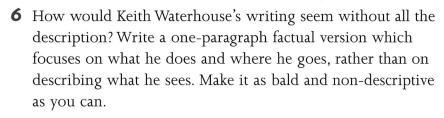

Image	The picture it creates
a Painted in a vivid red, like blood	
b The stew of tumbledown premises	
c The bisected veal, ham and egg pies	

6 How would Keith Waterhouse's writing seem without all the description? Write a one-paragraph factual version which focuses on what he does and where he goes, rather than on describing what he sees. Make it as bald and non-descriptive as you can.

Then write a sentence describing how you approached the task and what the final text is like.

WRITING ACTIVITY

Write a short, vivid description of a setting in your school – for example, a corridor at breaktime or the busy dining room. Focus on description, not plot or dialogue. Try to create a strong visual impression of what the place is like. You might:

- refer to sights, sounds and textures
- use imagery (similes and metaphor)
- use lists
- use long sentences, to create an impression of detailed description.

EXTENDED WRITING

Working with a partner, talk about your memories of people or places. One of you (Student A) should choose a person or location in your school that you both know – for example, a teacher or classroom. Don't tell your partner who or where it is.

Now Student B is allowed 15 questions to try to identify the person or place. Student A can only answer 'yes' or 'no'. Start with general questions: 'Is this a room?' 'Is it used for teaching?' Gradually make your questions more and more specific.

Now think back to a place that meant a lot to you as a child. It might be the house you were brought up in, your first school, or a den you liked to play in.

Write a vivid description of the place. Like Keith Waterhouse, imagine yourself back in that location, describing the scene to help the reader to visualize it.

You might:

* start with a general sentence ('The smell of the school is my strongest memory …')

* write in long sentences, full of detail

* use adjectives and adverbs

* use similes and metaphors

* use words relating to the senses

* focus on pure description, rather than telling a story.

Recounts: the essentials

Purpose and audience

Recounts tell us about events. They might include:

- autobiographies
- stories from history
- someone describing a crime he has just witnessed
- a newspaper story.

The audience may be familiar with the topic or writer, or it may all be new. It will usually be written in **chronological order** – that is, retelling the events in the sequence in which they happened.

Text level features

Most recounts will begin with an **opening paragraph** to set the scene, then give a description of events, and end with a **concluding paragraph**. Paragraphs will use **connectives** to link the sequence of ideas together.

Sentence level features

Recounts will usually use the **first person** (for stories and autobiography) or the **third person** (for factual reports). They are usually written in the **past tense**.

Often, there will be a variety of **sentence types** to create interest (e.g. several short sentences to build up suspense). Sometimes **dialogue** is used to move the story forward or to tell us more about a character.

Word level features

Recounts often aim to answer the questions: *who, where, when, what, why?* They may include descriptive writing, and techniques like **simile** and **metaphor** to create more vivid images. They may use words which are simple or complex, formal or informal, depending on what the writer is aiming to achieve.

Newspaper recount

Flying Solo

> ### OBJECTIVES
>
> This extract is an informal, entertaining newspaper report. You will study the following objectives:
>
> - Word level: *formality and word choice*
>
> - Sentence level: *complex sentences, variety of sentence structure, full range of punctuation, adapting text types,* and *degrees of formality*
>
> - Reading: *note-making formats, implied and explicit meanings,* and *development of key ideas*
>
> - Writing: *anticipate reader reaction, effective information, explain complex ideas,* and *formal description*
>
> - Speaking and listening: *commentary,* and *listen for a specific purpose*

Introduction

Newspapers are written to inform and entertain. Occasionally they also aim to persuade – for example, in their editorial articles, which are intended to shape the readers' opinions on important issues.

Newspapers also use a range of styles. News stories may be punchy, dramatic, detailed, serious or sensationalist; features writing may be more leisurely, reflective, and personal.

Here is an example of traditional news reporting, from the Sun. Look at the way the text aims to communicate information quickly and to entertain us. When you have finished studying it, you will write a newspaper article of your own.

FLYING SOLO

Exclusive by Jamie Pyatt

Plane with no pilot takes off at 70mph and crashes mile away

A plane hurtled down a runway and took off without a pilot after he hopped out for a few seconds to make a last-minute check.

Glyn Hughes left the light aircraft with its propeller spinning and its brakes on to look for an airfield official.

While his back was turned the plane trundled forward, did a U-turn, then sped along the runway at 70mph and took off.

Glyn dashed back to find the £35,000 Grumman AA-5A had vanished and told the airfield manager: 'Someone's nicked my plane.'

As cops raced to the scene another aircraft took off and spotted the Grumman wrecked in woods a mile away. The bizarre solo flight was revealed in a Civil Aviation Authority report into the crash at Canterbury Airfield, Kent.

It told how London businessman Glyn, 48, hired the aircraft from a Biggin Hill flying club for an afternoon.

Glyn, a pilot of eight years' experience, was about to make his return flight when he realised his battery was drained because

1. Pilot leaves cockpit to speak to security guard. When he returns 90 seconds later, plane has vanished

2. Empty plane moves forward, turns 180 degrees and takes off at 70mph

3. Crashes into ditch a mile away

he had left it on. So he and a security guard used a car battery to start the engine.

As he sat in the plane waiting for his battery to recharge he realised he had forgotten to refit its cover.

So, fearing a roasting from the flying club instructors, he decided to get out and look for it.

He left the brakes on but kept the engine running fearing the plane would not restart.

The report stated: 'He believed the security guard had the battery cover so he ran over to his caravan across the airfield.

'He reasoned he could be back in 90 seconds.

Character

'He found that the security guard did not know where the cover

was. When he returned the aircraft had gone.'

The plane had moved forward, turned left through 180 degrees, gathered speed and then taken off before crashing into a ditch.

The report does not reveal how it started moving on its own.

Glyn, a married dad of one who runs his own electronics business, was unavailable for comment.

Instructor Dave Lawrence said: 'It's a miracle no one was hurt. The airport is near houses and a motorway.'

One pilot said: 'Glyn's a colourful character who's had his share of incidents – I wouldn't lend him my plane.'

A spokeswoman for the plane's owners Civil Air said: 'I think we would all have found it really funny . . . if it had been someone else's plane.'

1. Pilot leaves cockpit to speak to security guard. When he returns 90 seconds later, plane has vanished.

2. Empty plane moves forward, turns 180 degrees and takes off at 70mph.

3. Crashes into ditch a mile away.

UNDERSTANDING THE TEXT

1 Where did the incident take place?

2 Why had the pilot left the plane?

3 What were his first thoughts when he noticed the plane had disappeared?

4 How were the whereabouts of the plane discovered?

5 What is the pilot's:

- ◆ name

- ◆ age

- ◆ family

- ◆ job?

6 Now look at the way the writer organizes the story. Which of the following questions does the article answer first: Who? When? What (happened)? Why? Where? Which of these questions gets answered last?

Put the five 'W' questions in the order in which they are answered in the article – 1 to 5.

INTERPRETING THE TEXT

7 Look at the diagram that accompanies the news story. Working in pairs, one person should use the diagram to explain to his or her partner exactly what happened with the aircraft. Make the explanation as clear as possible. The other person should listen and then say how clear the recount was. How could the speaker have structured the story more clearly?

8 Look at how much detail the picture adds to the story.

a Does the diagram contain all the essential pieces of information? Are there any other details you might have included?

b Do you think the diagram is important for fully understanding what happened? Explain why.

9 Throughout the story the writer refers to 'Glyn' (using his first name). Is this more or less formal than you might expect? What effect would it have had if the writer had referred to him as 'Hughes' or 'Mr Hughes'?

10 Towards the end of the article a pilot is quoted, talking about Glyn. Read what he says. What does he imply about Glyn and why the plane might have taken off without him?

LANGUAGE AND STRUCTURE

1 Look more closely at the headline. Even if this wasn't printed in large lettering, you would probably know that it is a newspaper headline. What features does it have which are typical of news headlines?

You might comment on:

♦ punctuation

♦ choice of vocabulary

♦ words that are left out.

2 News stories usually start with a topic sentence, which sets the tone of the story. Why do you think the writer uses the verb 'hurtled' in this topic sentence? Think of another verb he might have used.

3 Look at the fifth paragraph. Why do you think the writer says 'cops' rather than 'police'?

4 a What other examples are there of informal and vivid language?

b What do these examples of informal and vivid vocabulary tell you about the writer's view of his audience? What does he think they want from the newspaper?

5 Look more closely at the way the writer uses punctuation to help the reader understand his story. Use the questions below to comment on some punctuation used in this text.

a In the first paragraph, why does the writer place a hyphen between 'last' and 'minute'? Would it make any difference if the hyphen were left out?

> HINT
>
> ● 'Minute' can be pronounced in two different ways to give different meanings

b Look at the start of this sentence:

Glyn, a pilot of eight years' experience, was about to make his return flight . . .

Explain why the writer uses two commas around the phrase 'a pilot of eight years' experience'. Can you think of a different way he might have written the same ideas, using full stops rather than commas?

c Look at this sentence:

One pilot said: 'Glyn's a colourful character who's had his share of incidents – I wouldn't lend him my plane.'

Why do you think the writer has chosen to separate the ideas with a dash rather than a full stop? What effect does it have?

6 This activity helps you with note-making skills. Use a form like the one below to build up a picture of what happened to the mysterious aircraft. Fill it in using details from the *Sun* article.

Self-Flying Aircraft Factsheet

What do we know about what happened, where and when?

What _____

Where _____

When _____

What do we know about the person in control of the plane?

What questions are left unanswered?

WRITING ACTIVITY

The *Sun* article reports the story with a tone of fascination about what happened. In places, it has a jokey tone. But people living close to the airfield might take a more serious view.

Write a more formal newspaper report of the events. Imagine that your article is appearing in a local newspaper where readers will be seriously worried by what has happened, and concerned that nothing like it should happen again.

Your aim should be to inform readers about what has happened rather than to entertain them. Remember that this type of newspaper report uses the third person and the past tense, and aims to answer the questions: *who, where, when, what, why?*

a Think of a headline.

b Think of a topic sentence.

c Retell the story in 200 words, keeping the tone formal.

Think about:

♦ which information you will include (about the event, the plane, the pilot)

♦ how you will keep the tone of your story factual

♦ how you will show that this was a very dangerous event.

When you have finished, read through your work and think carefully about the effect it will have on the reader. Revise it if necessary, to make sure it gives clear information.

6 Personal recount
Going Surfing

OBJECTIVES

Using comic effects in a recount is an important way of entertaining the reader, as this extract shows. These are the objectives you will study:

- Word level: *formality and word choice*, and *ironic use of words*

- Sentence level: *variety of sentence structure*, *adapting text types*, and *degree of formality*

- Reading: *implied and explicit meanings*, and *transposition* (how meanings are changed when information is presented in different forms)

- Writing: *establish the tone*, *effective information*, and *formal description*

Introduction

Bill Bryson is well known for his comic travel writing. He visits places and then describes the people, customs, and his own experiences there in a way that is designed to make us laugh. Sometimes the comedy is in the things that happen to him; at other times, it is the tone of voice he uses – mixing confusion, fear, dislike and a strong feeling of not being quite in control of a situation.

When you have studied this entertaining recount, you can practise writing one of your own.

The extract is from Bill Bryson's account of his visit to Australia, *Down Under*. His guides are an Australian journalist, Deirdre Macken, and a young photographer named Glenn Hunt. They offer to take him boogie boarding …

GLOSSARY

Evasively – *as if hiding the full truth*

Abraded – *scraped*

Unprepossessing – *unattractive*

Going Surfing

'What is boogie boarding exactly?'

'Oh, it's fun. You'll love it,' Deirdre said breezily but, I thought, just a touch evasively.

'Yes, but what is it?'

'It's an aquatic sport. It's heaps of fun. Isn't it heaps of fun, Glenn?'

'But what does it entail exactly?' I persisted.

'You take a kind of miniature surfboard and paddle out into the sea, where you catch a big wave and ride it back to shore. It's easy. You'll love it.'

'What about sharks?' I asked uneasily.

'Oh, there's hardly any sharks here. Glenn, how long has it been since someone was killed by a shark?'

'Oh, ages,' Glenn said, considering. 'Couple of months at least.'

'Couple of months?' I squeaked.

'At least. Sharks are way overrated as a danger,' Glenn added. 'Way overrated. It's the rips that'll most likely get yer.' He returned to taking pictures.

'Rips?'

'Underwater currents that run at an angle to the shore and sometimes carry people out to sea,' Deirdre explained. 'But don't worry. That won't happen to you.'

'Why?'

'Because we're here to look after you.' She smiled serenely, drained her cup and reminded us that we needed to keep moving.

Three hours later, our other activities completed, we stood on a remote-seeming strand at a place called Freshwater Beach, near Manly. …

Urged on by Deirdre, who seemed keen as anything to get into the briny drink, we began to strip down – slowly and deliberatively in my case, eagerly in hers – to the swimsuits she had instructed us to wear beneath our clothes.

'If you're caught in a rip,' Deirdre was saying, 'the trick is not to panic.'

I looked at her. 'You're telling me to drown calmly?'

'No, no. Just keep your wits. Don't try to swim against the current. Swim across it. And if you're still in trouble, just wave your arm like this' – she gave the kind of big, languorous wave that only an Australian could possibly consider an appropriate response to a death-at-sea situation – 'and wait for the lifeguard to come.'

'What if the lifeguard doesn't see me?'

'He'll see you.'

'But what if he doesn't?'

But Deirdre was already wading into the surf, a boogie board tucked under her arm. …

Let me just pause here for a moment to interpose two small stories. In 1935, not far from where we stood now, some fishermen captured a fourteen-foot beige shark and took it to a public aquarium at Coogee, where it was put on display. The shark swam around for a day or two in its new home, then abruptly, and to the certain surprise of the viewing public, regurgitated a human arm. When last seen the arm had been attached to a young man named Jimmy Smith, who had, I've no doubt, signalled his predicament with a big, languorous wave.

Now my second story. Three years later, on a clear, bright, calm

Sunday afternoon at Bondi Beach, also not far from where we now stood, from out of nowhere there came four freak waves, each up to twenty-five feet high. More than 200 people were carried out to sea in the undertow. Fortunately, fifty lifeguards were in attendance that day, and they managed to save all but six people. I am aware that we are talking about incidents that happened many years ago. I don't care. My point remains: the ocean is a treacherous place.

Sighing, I shuffled into the pale green and cream-flecked water. The bay was surprisingly shallow. We trudged perhaps 100 feet out and it was still only a little over our knees, though even here there was an extraordinarily powerful current – strong enough to pull you off your feet if you weren't real vigilant. Another fifty feet on, where the water rose over our waists, the waves were breaking. … I have almost no experience of the sea, and I found it frankly disconcerting to be wading into a

rollercoaster of water. Deirdre shrieked with pleasure.

Then she showed me how the boogie board works. It was promisingly simple in principle. As a wave passed, she would leap aboard and skim along on its crest for many yards. Then Glenn had a turn and went even further. There is no question that it looked like fun. It didn't look too hard either. I was tentatively eager to have a try.

I positioned myself for the first wave, then jumped aboard and sank like an anvil.

'How'd you do that?' asked Glenn in wonder.

'No idea.'

I repeated the exercise with the same result.

'Amazing,' he said.

There followed a half hour in which the two of them watched first with guarded amusement, then a kind of astonishment, and finally something not unlike pity,

as I repeatedly vanished beneath the waves and was scraped over an area of ocean floor roughly the size of Polk County, Iowa. After a variable but lengthy period, I would surface, gasping and confused, at a point anywhere from four feet to a mile and a quarter distant, and be immediately carried under again by a following wave. …

Perhaps it was the oxygen deprivation, but I was rather lost in my own little world when Deirdre grabbed my arm just before I was about to go under again and said in a husky tone: 'Look out! There's a bluey.'

Glenn took on an immediate expression of alarm. 'Where?'

'What's a bluey?' I asked, appalled to discover that there was some additional danger I hadn't been told about.

'A bluebottle,' she explained and pointed to a small jellyfish of the type (as I later learned from browsing through a fat book titled,

if I recall, *Things That Will Kill You Horridly in Australia: Volume 19*) known elsewhere as a Portuguese man-of-war. I squinted at it as it drifted past. It looked unprepossessing, like a blue condom with strings attached.

'Is it dangerous?' I asked.

Now before we hear Deirdre's response to me as I stood there, vulnerable and abraded, shivering, nearly naked and half drowned, let me just quote from her subsequent article in the Herald:

While the photographer shoots, Bryson and boogie board are dragged 40 metres down the beach in a rip. The shore rip runs south to north, unlike the rip further out which runs north to south. Bryson doesn't know this. He didn't read the warning sign on the beach. Nor does he know about the bluebottle being blown in his direction – now less than a metre away – a swollen stinger that could give him 20 minutes of agony and, if he's unlucky, an unsightly allergic reaction to carry on his torso for life.

'Dangerous? No,' Deirdre replied now as we stood gawping at the bluebottle. 'But don't brush against it.'

'Why not?'

'Might be a bit uncomfortable.' ...

'Hey, there's another one,' said Glenn.

We watched another one drift by. Deirdre was scanning the water.

'Sometimes they come in waves,' she said. 'Might be an idea to get out of the water.'

I didn't need to be told twice.

UNDERSTANDING THE TEXT

1 How can you tell that Bill Bryson is nervous about boogie boarding?

2 What happens to him when he first tries to surf?

3 How can you tell from Glenn's reaction that 'bluebottles' are dangerous?

4 Why do you think Deirdre does not tell him the full truth about the 'bluebottle'?

INTERPRETING THE TEXT

5 As you read the text, you probably didn't expect that Bill Bryson would be able to surf successfully. How does his ironic tone help us guess in advance that his attempts will be unsuccessful?

HINT

● Look at sentences such as 'It was promisingly simple in principle'

6 Which parts of the text did you find funniest, and why?

LANGUAGE AND STRUCTURE

1 a Look at the first section of the text. This sets the situation up for what happens later. Look at the range of sentence functions the writer uses. Try to find an example of:

- a statement

- a question

- an imperative (or command)

- a minor sentence (a sentence without a verb).

b In this early section, how does the use of questions make us want to read on?

2 The later sections use some complex sentences to explain the action. Find an example of a complex sentence that packs in a lot of detail.

3 Although recounts are often written in chronological order, Bill Bryson covers a number of time sequences in this extract. The first section describes him first hearing about boogie boarding. The next section moves forward in time three hours. Then he goes back in time for accounts of events in 1935 and 1938, before continuing with the description of his time at the beach.

a Find the connecting words which he uses to show the shifts to different times.

b How might he have introduced the flashback to 1935 in a different way?

c How does this use of different time sequences help to create humour?

4 Like many humorous writers, Bill Bryson uses similes and exaggeration, like this:

Simile

It looked unprepossessing, like a blue condom with strings attached

Exaggeration

I was scraped over an area of ocean floor roughly the size of Polk County, Iowa

He also uses some memorable phrasing, with metaphors like this:

… wading into a rollercoaster of water.

Each of these techniques adds to the comic effect. Find a sentence or phrase using one of these techniques, which you think is particularly effective. Write it down, and comment on why you think it adds humour to the text.

5 Look at the newspaper account Deirdre Macken writes. Her style is quite different from Bill Bryson's and also comic. How does she write differently from him? You might mention:

- the length of her sentences
- whether she uses the same range of sentences as Bill Bryson
- the way she describes Bryson's character
- the way she describes things he has not done
- whether her account is more formal or informal.

WRITING ACTIVITY

Based on reading of this extract, what do you think are some of the secrets of successful comic writing?

Write an advice sheet for students, giving five tips on how to write humorous non-fiction (such as autobiography and travel writing).

You might mention:

- how to structure ideas so that it builds anticipation for later parts of the storyline
- using similes and metaphors
- using exaggeration
- using memorable phrasing
- how to present people in the writing
- how to use dialogue.

Extended Writing

In threes, talk about any embarrassing incidents you have been involved in, such as:

♦ an embarrassing time on holiday

♦ a day you were in trouble at school

♦ an event with your own relatives.

Take it in turns to say what happened, quickly telling the story to the others. Now choose one of these events and use it as the opening for a piece of comic writing. Refer back to the hints you wrote down in the Writing Activity on page 55.

♦ Use a detached tone like Bill Bryson – as if you have stepped outside yourself to describe what is happening (e.g. 'My brain was telling me this was fine; my body didn't believe a word and just wanted to get out of there.')

♦ Use a variety of sentences (including questions).

♦ Give details about people and places.

♦ Use dialogue to add humour.

Read your account aloud to other people. Talk about how you have each tried to create humour. Discuss the ways in which the written accounts feel different from the spoken versions with which you started the task.

What is autobiography?

Purpose and audience

Recounts tell readers about events that have happened. We have already seen them in newspapers and in personal accounts.

Autobiographies are important examples of recounts. They describe the events that have taken place in someone's own life. Usually, they will aim to entertain the reader.

Text level features

Most autobiography is written in a **chronological** sequence (placing events in the order in which they happened).

It is important to remember, however, that autobiographies often reflect the **personality** of the writer: they might change the conventions or rules of writing to suit themselves. For example, in his autobiography *Timebends*, the playwright Arthur Miller does not use a chronological sequence. Instead, he moves backwards and forwards over events in his life.

Sentence level features

Autobiographies use the **first person** ('I' and 'me'). They aim to paint a picture with words in order to help the reader visualize the scenes and events from the writer's life. **Connectives** like *then*, *later*, *next* will be used to link the ideas together and show the movement of time.

Word level features

Autobiographical writing will often use very descriptive language, and techniques such as **similes** and **metaphors**. It usually aims to answer the questions *who, what, where, when, why?*

Autobiographical recount
Healing the Horses

OBJECTIVES

In this extract, the writer gives an account of his own experiences in a form that reads like a novel. You will learn about the following objectives:

- Word level: *unfamiliar words* (working out their meaning), and *formality and word choice*

- Sentence level: *adapting text types*, and *standard English and dialect*

- Reading: *note-making formats*, *versatile reading* (using a range of reading strategies), and *transposition* (how meanings are changed when information is presented in different forms)

- Writing: *effective planning*, *effective information*, and *formal description*

Introduction

James Herriott's reflections on his career as a country vet became a huge hit when they were published in the 1970s, leading to television series and a film.

They read like novels, but they are based largely on the vet's own real-life experiences. In this extract, he has been called out to look at some old shire horses. The name 'James Herriott' is part of the writer's technique – it is a character's name, not his real name, which he kept secret through to his retirement.

When you have studied the text, you will write a record yourself.

GLOSSARY

Gelding – *male horse*

Roan – *horse that has a coat sprinkled with white or grey*

Venerable – *impressive and elderly*

Excoriating – *removing skin from*

Healing the Horses

I was glad when we reached the flat land at the bottom. My arms seemed to have been stretched by several inches and I could feel a trickle of sweat on my brow. Old John appeared unaffected; he flicked the fork from his shoulder and the bale thudded on to the grass.

The two horses turned towards us at the sound. They were standing fetlock deep in the pebbly shallows just beyond a little beach which merged into the green carpet of turf; nose to tail, they had been rubbing their chins gently along each other's backs, unconscious of our approach. A high cliff overhanging the far bank made a perfect wind break while on either side of us clumps of oak blazed in the autumn sunshine.

'They're in a nice spot, Mr Skipton,' I said.

'Aye, they can keep cool in the hot weather and they've got the barn when winter comes.' John pointed to a low, thick-walled building with a single door. 'They can come and go as they please.'

The sound of his voice brought the horses out of the river at a stiff trot and as they came near you could see they really were old. The mare was a chestnut and the gelding was a light bay but their coats were so flecked with grey that they almost looked like roans. This was most pronounced on their faces where the sprinkling of white hairs, the sunken eyes and the deep cavity above the eyes gave them a truly venerable appearance.

For all that, they capered around John with a fair attempt at skittishness, stamping their feet, throwing their heads about, pushing his cap over his eyes with their muzzles.

'Get by, leave off!' he shouted. 'Daft awd beggars.' But he tugged absently at the mare's forelock and ran his hand briefly along the neck of the gelding.

'When did they last do any work?' I asked.

'Oh, about twelve years ago, I reckon.'

I stared at John. 'Twelve years! And have they been down here all that time?'

'Aye, just lakin' about down here, retired like. They've earned it an' all.' For a few moments he stood silent, shoulders hunched, hands deep in the pockets of his coat, then he spoke quietly as if to himself. 'They were two slaves when I was a slave.' He turned and looked at me and for a revealing moment I read in the pale blue eyes something of the agony and struggle he had shared with the animals.

'But twelve years! How old are they, anyway?'

John's mouth twisted up at one corner. 'Well you're t'vet. You tell me.'

I stepped forward confidently, my mind buzzing with Galvayne's groove, shape of marks, degree of slope and the rest; I grasped the unprotesting upper lip of the mare and looked at her teeth.

'Good God!' I gasped. 'I've never seen anything like this.' The incisors were immensely long and projecting forward till they met at an angle of about forty-five degrees. There were no marks at all – they had long since gone.

I laughed and turned back to the old man. 'It's no good, I'd only be guessing. You'll have to tell me.'

'Well she's about thirty and gelding's a year or two younger. She's had fifteen grand foals and never ailed owt except a bit of teeth trouble. We've had them rasped a time or two and it's time they were done again, I reckon. They're both losing ground and dropping bits of half chewed hay from their mouths. Gelding's the worst – has a right job champin' his grub.'

I put my hand into the mare's mouth, grasped her tongue and pulled it out to one side. A quick exploration of the molars with my other hand

revealed what I suspected; the outside edges of the upper teeth were overgrown and jagged and were irritating the cheeks while the inside edges of the lower molars were in a similar state and were slightly excoriating the tongue.

'I'll soon make her more comfortable, Mr Skipton. With those sharp edges rubbed off she'll be as good as new.' I got the rasp out of my vast box, held the tongue in one hand and worked the rough surface along the teeth, checking occasionally with my fingers till the points had been sufficiently reduced.

'That's about right,' I said after a few minutes. 'I don't want to make them too smooth or she won't be able to grind her food.'

John grunted. 'Good enough. Now have a look at t'other. There's summat far wrong with him.'

I had a feel at the gelding's teeth. 'Just the same as the mare. Soon put him right, too.'

But pushing at the rasp, I had an uncomfortable feeling that something was not quite right. The thing wouldn't go fully to the back of the mouth; something was stopping it. I stopped rasping and explored again, reaching with my fingers as far as I could. And I came upon something very strange, something which shouldn't have been there at all. It was like a great chunk of bone projecting down from the roof of the mouth.

It was time I had a proper look. I got out my pocket torch and shone it over the back of the tongue. It was easy to see the trouble now; the last upper molar was overlapping the lower one resulting in a gross overgrowth of the posterior border. The result was a sabre-like barb about three inches long stabbing down into the tender tissue of the gum.

That would have to come off – right now. My jauntiness vanished and I suppressed a shudder; it meant using the horrible shears – those great long-handled things with the screw operated by a cross bar. They gave me the willies because I am one of those people who can't bear to watch anybody blowing up a balloon and this was the same sort of thing only worse. You fastened the sharp blades of the shears on to the tooth and began to turn the bar slowly, slowly. Soon the tooth began to groan and creak under the tremendous leverage and you knew that any second it would break off and when it did it was like somebody letting off a rifle in your ear. That was when all hell usually broke loose but mercifully this was a quiet old horse and I wouldn't expect him to start dancing around on his hind legs. There was no pain for the horse because the overgrown part had no nerve supply – it was the noise that caused the trouble.

Returning to my crate I produced the dreadful instrument and with it a Haussman's gag which I inserted on the incisors and opened on its ratchet till the mouth gaped wide. Everything was easy to see then and, of course, there it was – a great prong at the other side of the mouth exactly like the first. Great, great, now I had two to chop off.

The old horse stood patiently, eyes almost closed, as though he had seen it all and nothing in the world was going to bother him. I went through the motions with my toes curling and when the sharp crack came, the white-bordered eyes opened wide, but only in mild surprise. He never even moved. When I did the other side he paid no attention at all; in fact, with the gag prising his jaws apart he looked exactly as though he was yawning with boredom.

As I bundled the tools away, John picked up the bony spicules from the grass and studied them with interest. 'Well, poor awd beggar. Good job I got you along, young man. Reckon he'll feel a lot better now.'

UNDERSTANDING THE TEXT

Before examining the writer's techniques, look more closely at the facts in his account. You will need to read for meaning in different ways to do this.

1 How can you tell that the journey to reach the horses has been hard work for the narrator?

2 What signs are there that the horses are old?

3 How do the horses show that they like Mr Skipton?

4 What is the problem with the first horse's mouth?

5 What is the problem with the second horse's mouth?

INTERPRETING THE TEXT

Having looked at the facts in the text, now look at other meanings and at the writer's style.

6 Look at the men's conversation about how long it is since the horses last did any work. What is implied about Mr Skipton's past experiences, and his feelings for the horses?

7 What impression do you get of James Herriott from the extract? Think about:

   ◆ how he gets on with Mr Skipton

   ◆ how he deals with the horses' problems

   ◆ how he speaks.

8 The text is based on real-life people and events. But would it be possible to see it purely as a made-up story? What features do you notice in this autobiographical writing which you might also expect in fiction (for example, a novel set in the countryside)? Aim to find two features.

LANGUAGE AND STRUCTURE

1 While James Herriott speaks in standard English, Mr Skipton uses a number of Yorkshire dialect words and structures.

a Find a word he uses which we would not expect to find in standard English.

b Write down what you think the word means.

2 Now look again at James Herriott's own spoken words – such as: 'They're in a nice spot, Mr Skipton.' Which of the following statements do you think best explains the way the writer presents his own language?

a The way James Herriott speaks shows that he comes from a different background from Mr Skipton.

b It shows that James Herriott is an outsider in this area – he does not belong here.

c James Herriott celebrates the way people speak in their own dialects.

d James Herriott is presented as 'posh' in his language.

Write a sentence explaining your choice.

3 Yorkshire dialect also uses certain phrases and structures, like these:

retired like   an' all   t'other (rather than 'the other')

Take the following three examples and write them in the standard English dialect used by James Herriott:

a 'Aye, just lakin' about down here, retired like.'

b 'They've earned it an' all.'

c 'Now have a look at t'other.'

4 Think about the way you have rewritten the dialect expressions in standard English for question 3. Try to describe how you can tell the difference between Yorkshire dialect and standard English. Use the list below to help you – it gives some examples of the ways different dialects may vary from standard English.

◆ Irregular agreement between subject and verb (e.g. *we was*).

◆ Irregular formation of the past tense (e.g. it **were** finished).

◆ Different vocabulary from standard English (e.g. *bairn* instead of *child*).

◆ Phrases which we would not find in standard English.

◆ Different use of pronouns and prepositions (e.g. *we saw **them** horses*).

◆ Running two words of standard English together to make a new word (e.g. *we saw **t'old** man*).

Start your comment like this:

Example a) seems like regional dialect rather than standard English because ...

WRITING ACTIVITY

James Herriott writes in a vivid personal style. How would his recount be different if it were a record of his work for the day, rather than an autobiography?

Imagine you are James Herriott and you have to keep a record of:

a the visits you make

b the problems the animals have

c the way you treat them.

Make some notes on the information you will include. Then write a short extract (one paragraph) for this record. Remember that the style will be more impersonal and less descriptive. You might start like this:

Thursday 23/8/01

Visit to Mr Skipton's farm. 2 old shire horses. Problem:

When you have finished, write a sentence or short paragraph describing the main similarities and differences between the style of your recount and the James Herriott autobiography.

Personal recount

Relative Values

OBJECTIVES

This extract gives a very personal view of a period in the writer's life.
These are the objectives you will be studying:

- Word level: *prepositions and connectives*, and *formality and word choice*

- Sentence level: *variety of sentence structure, colons and semi-colons, grouping sentences*, and *cohesion and coherence*

- Reading: *trace developments* (of themes and values), and *bias and objectivity*

- Writing: *effective information*, and *formal description*

Introduction

Autobiography is an important type of text to consider when we are looking at recounts.

Many people think that autobiographical writing comes only in books describing a person's whole life. In fact, a lot of writing in newspapers, letters and journals is also autobiographical. It often focuses on one or two key moments from a writer's life.

The *Sunday Times* series 'Relative Values' does this. It invites people to talk about their relationship with a member of their family, and the way this has shaped who they are.

This example is written by the singer Des'ree. After looking at her recount, you can write one of your own.

GLOSSARY

Okra – *a tropical plant used as a vegetable*

Apprehensive – *worried about what might happen*

Antipathy – *the opposite of sympathy: rivalry and dislike*

Relative Values

I grew up in a happy household in southeast London. My parents appeared to be very happy together, there was lots of love and laughter, parties and music. My mum's laugh used to remind me of sunshine; it was always bright and crisp, and it used to touch me.

Dad was born in Barbados and came over here in the 1960s to study accountancy; my mother came over from Guyana at the same time to study nursing. My father was quiet, very reserved, and left most things up to my mother, who was highly ambitious and wanted the best for her family. She really pushed and encouraged my father. That was a pattern in his life. He had very domineering parents. As a boy he was a talented cricketer – Sir Gary Sobers came to his school and asked the headmaster if he could play for the West Indies. But his parents felt cricket wasn't a stable occupation, that he should be academic and go to university, and wouldn't allow it.

Dad's main loves in life when I was a child were cricket and jazz. Every Saturday he would get together with his West Indian friends and cook traditional West Indian food, particularly *coucou*,

which is the national dish of Barbados, a stew of cornmeal and okra served with flying fish. It was a ritual my Dad loved; there would be jazz music in the background, and they'd talk all night about cricket and make jokes, and it kept up his links with his homeland.

After my parents had lived in Britain for 20 years, they wanted my sister and me to experience the West Indies, so we upped sticks and moved to Barbados. My dad seemed happy and relaxed there, meeting his old buddies, and of course he fitted straight in because it was the country of his birth and his relatives were there. My mum was a little more apprehensive. We lived in my father's parents' home, which she was never really happy about, and they weren't very keen on my mum, to be honest, because she wasn't from the island. It's the small-island, big-island thing – there is a natural antipathy between the Bajans and the Guyanans.

So Mum wanted to have her own home, and she put pressure on my dad to find somewhere else for us to live, but he saw no reason to move from the family home. He felt it was big enough,

he was happy there – basically, any excuse. Meanwhile, I noticed that the happy times in our family unit were becoming much more rare. There was less talk. Then there was no talking at all. My parents didn't pretend everything was okay – my mother has always been very open. She said: 'Daddy and I are going through a difficult period, but don't be alarmed by it, this is what happens sometimes within a marriage, and you have to work things through.'

I suppose my sister and I didn't really take in what was happening because at the end of the day we felt, that's adult business, they'll deal with it, because parents take care of everything. But I remember looking at my father after that conversation, and I looked at him in a different way. He was always so quiet, I thought: 'What's going on in your mind? Why don't you throw a tantrum, *do* something, Daddy!' My attitude towards him changed then, because I saw he was weak, and we don't expect our parents to be weak, we expect them to be pillars of strength. So I started to feel jittery, because I knew that the link, the connection, was about to be severed, and when I felt things starting to crumble it tore me apart.

He retreated. He found it very difficult to talk to us. It could have been guilt, it could have been a number of things, but I stopped communicating with him then because he had become like a stranger to me.

One day Mum sat us down in the kitchen. 'Your father and I are no longer going to be together,' she said. 'We're going to get a divorce.' She was very composed then, because she wanted to be

composed for us. My sister and I burst out crying, there were lots of tears. But I was the eldest, and I realised I had to step into my dad's position. I had to be the strong one, because I wouldn't want Mum to think there was nobody there for her.

Dad stayed in the house until it was time for us to go back to England. I can remember saying goodbye to him; it was like looking at a stranger. I remember my sister and my mother crying, but I didn't shed a tear, and I was angry at them for crying. Maybe that was just my way of coping. I was like a pillar of steel, I refused to be moved by the whole thing and detached myself. In a way, I felt sorry for him because I thought: 'We're going to be okay, but I don't know what's going to happen to you.'

Dad stayed on in the Caribbean. My mother always encouraged us to keep in contact, either by phone or by letter, which I did for her sake – not for my own, because I was still angry. It was 10 years later when my father came to London. We went to see him at the airport, and I was surprised by how much he had changed. We were shocked at his appearance: he looked so much older, he seemed very

weary. He wouldn't really convey anything to us. 'Oh, I'm fine,' he said, 'a little trouble with my eyes and my blood pressure.' But that was it. Nothing deeper.

The most significant time I've spent with my father was when my sister and I went to St Lucia on holiday with him last Christmas. We were together for five weeks and we were finally able to talk to him. My sister is a psychologist, so she was able to extract things from him that I couldn't, and it was as though I was getting to know him for the first time – his likes, his dislikes, his goals, his dreams, his fears.

I didn't hold back. I said how angry we were, how rejected we had felt, I just kind of laid it out. He took it quietly; maybe he hadn't anticipated that I would tell him that. Not that everything is happy ever after, because he wasn't able to balm those wounds. But I'm not angry any more. I realise now that my father was one of those people who are too easy-going. He regretted not playing for the West Indies cricket team, he regretted certain other opportunities in his life he didn't take because he didn't have the guts to jump in and take the risk, and that included the marriage.

UNDERSTANDING THE TEXT

1 Write down two facts we learn from the article about her parents' background – one about Des'ree's mother and another about her father.

2 Why did the family move to Barbados?

3 Why did the father's family not get on with Des'ree's mother?

4 How did Des'ree's attitude to her father change in Barbados?

5 When did Des'ree last see her father?

INTERPRETING THE TEXT

6 How can you tell that Des'ree's family is important to her?

7 By the end of the article she says: 'I'm not angry any more.' How has her understanding of her father changed? Can we see this change developing as her recount goes along?

8 How would you describe the tone of the writer?

bitter   angry   disappointed   resentful   accepting

Write down the word that you think is most suitable, and then write a sentence explaining why you have chosen it.

9 Some people might say that Des'ree's recount seems biased rather than factual – that it is impossible for her to describe her life and family in an objective way. Do you agree or disagree? Say why.

10 Personal recounts tend to contain both facts and opinions. Use a table like the one below to sort out the differences between facts and opinions in this text.

Facts about her father	Opinions about her father
Facts about her mother	Opinions about her mother
Facts about Des'ree	

Why don't we gain any direct opinions of Des'ree herself?

LANGUAGE AND STRUCTURE

1 Some parts of Des'ree's text feel quite formal; other parts seem informal.

  a Find three examples of formal words or phrases and three of informal ones. Try to explain why you think they are formal or informal. An example is done for you.

Formal style

Example: *there is a natural antipathy*

Comment: **antipathy** *is an unfamiliar, technical word.*

Informal style

Example: *so we upped sticks and moved to Barbados*

Comment: **upped sticks** *is a chatty expression which you might use in spoken English rather than a written text.*

  b The writer refers to her parents as 'Mum' and 'Dad'. What effect would it have if she used the phrases 'my mother' and 'my father' instead?

2 Des'ree uses a variety of sentences and joins them together with connectives. Her recount moves backwards and forwards in time. At the start of some paragraphs she uses connectives to help the reader follow the sequence of her writing.

Look at these three examples of connectives used at the beginning of paragraphs, and describe the purpose of each one. Use the prompt list on the next page to help you.

Example of connective	Purpose of the connective
After (paragraph 4)	
So (paragraph 5)	
One day (paragraph 8)	

Possible purposes of connectives

- to move us back in time

- to give an illustration or example

- to show the effect of something that has happened

- to move us forward in time

- to summarize or generalize

- to move to a different setting.

3 Look at the two examples below, where Des'ree uses semi-colons within her sentences:

Dad was born in Barbados and came over here in the 1960s to study accountancy; my mother came over from Guyana at the same time to study nursing.

He took it quietly; maybe he hadn't anticipated that I would tell him that.

a How would the effect have been different if Des'ree had used a full stop instead of the semi-colon?

b How does the semi-colon help Des'ree to express her meaning more precisely?

WRITING ACTIVITY

Although the text is chiefly about Des'ree and her feelings, we also learn quite a lot about her parents. Imagine you are Des'ree's father. Retell some of the text from his point of view. Structure it like this:

- your background and early life in Britain

- why you decided to return to Barbados

- how you felt that things went wrong

- how you feel now about your relationship with Des'ree.

Aim to show the father's point of view, helping the reader to understand what he is like. Remember to use the first person, set events in chronological order, link your ideas with connectives, and use descriptive words to help your reader visualize the scenes.

EXTENDED WRITING

Write a short piece for your own autobiography. You might choose a comic scene, when something funny happened to you, or a moving one, like Des'ree's.

Start by making notes on the moment you will describe. These might include:

◆ describing a place where you used to live

◆ recalling memories of parents or a friend

◆ recounting an incident that happened at school.

Brainstorm details of people, places, time, and any colours, smells or other fragments of memory you have.

Think about how personal your style will be. Then plan how you will organize your autobiographical writing. Will you use chronological order, or move backwards and forwards in time?

Think of connectives you might use to link sentences and paragraphs into a clear sequence for readers to follow.

Aim to produce 3-5 paragraphs of concentrated autobiographical writing.

Information texts: the essentials

Purpose and audience

Information texts describe how things are. They might include reference books, dictionaries, textbooks, factsheets, and leaflets.

The audience will be people who want to know more about the topic. They may already have some knowledge of the subject.

Information texts will be clear, well-ordered, and easy to follow.

Text level features

Information texts will often use **headings** to break the information up into different sections, and use **layout features** such as tables and diagrams to help make the information clear.

They might start with **general facts** and then go into more **detail**. Often they use a **non-chronological order** – they place information in order of importance, not the order that events take place.

Sentence level features

Information texts will usually use:

◆ the **third-person** form, to create an impersonal tone

◆ the **present tense**

◆ the **passive voice** ('salmon are farmed in large tanks' rather than 'people farm salmon in large tanks')

◆ a mix of **simple and compound sentences**

◆ **questions** addressed to the reader, to involve the reader more.

Word level features

Information texts will often use very precise terms, and sometimes **technical language**. This will depend on how much the writer thinks the reader knows about the topic. The writers of information texts avoid using much descriptive language. They will emphasize **facts**, using nouns and verbs in order to describe processes, and the text will usually be formal.

Technical information
Exploded Drawings

Introduction

Information texts are often aimed at people who know something about a subject, but may need to find out more. These texts are often designed to be used for reference – for those times when you need to look for more information about a topic or process. This means that clarity is most important. The best information texts don't use just language to inform the reader – they will use layout too.

This is a page from a textbook used by students studying Design Technology. This page is about 'exploded drawings'. Examine the way it presents information. It is aimed at an audience aged 15–16. When you have studied this text, you can practise presenting the information yourself.

6.4 EXPLODED DRAWINGS

BY THE END OF THIS SPREAD, YOU SHOULD BE ABLE TO:

■ produce exploded drawings

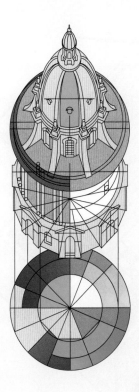

Illustration 4

Exploded drawings help the designer or manufacturer explain to the user how a product is assembled.

Exploded drawings are three-dimensional drawings. They are usually drawn using perspective.

It is important that the drawings of the individual parts of a product are separated so that the viewer can easily mentally assemble them. If the exploded parts are too close together or too far apart, it becomes more difficult to do this.

Illustrations 1, 2 & 3 show three exploded illustrations of three familiar components – a bolt, a washer and a nut. Which illustration do you think would be most helpful to a young child assembling the three parts?

We can also produce vertically drawn exploded views of the same components (Illustration 4).

The following illustration has been drawn using a different exploded drawing method.

Illustration 1

Illustration 2

Illustration 3

As you can see, it is useful to 'raise the roof' of a building to allow the viewer to look inside. This exposes aspects of the interior planning or layout.

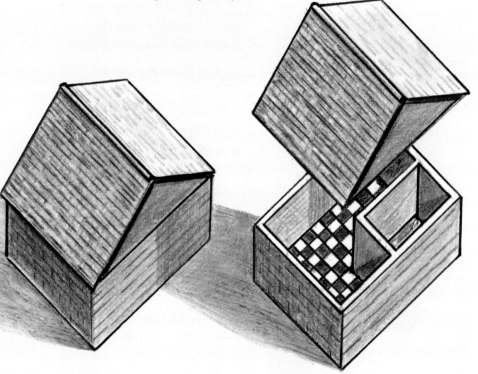

A model of a single-storey building

52

UNDERSTANDING THE TEXT

1 What is an exploded drawing for?

2 How does the writer help readers to know what they should have learned by the end of the unit?

3 Why do the drawings need to show the separate parts of objects?

4 Look at the formal words below. Think of a different word or phrase that the writer might have used:

   a *how a product is* **assembled**

   b *views of the same* **components**.

INTERPRETING THE TEXT

5 In information texts, paragraphs are often organized so that each contains one piece of information. Look at the structure of this text. It is written in short paragraphs. Use a grid like the one below to say what each of these paragraphs is about.

Paragraph	Topic
1	
2	
3	
4	
5	

6 Using your completed grid to help you, decide which of these statements (a–d) you most agree with.

   a The text gives a lot of examples of exploded drawings.

   b The text starts with an example of an exploded drawing, and then shows how these can work in other subject areas.

   c The first paragraph introduces the topic. The second gives more detail. The rest of the paragraphs provide examples.

d The first paragraph introduces the topic. Paragraphs 2 and 3 give more information. Paragraph 4 gets the reader thinking about examples. Paragraph 5 gives a further example.

Write a sentence explaining your choice.

7 On a scale of 1 (low) to 5 (high), how helpful do you find the layout of the page in making the information clear? Write a sentence saying how you think the layout could be improved.

8 Think about the audience for this text. Is it aimed at people who know very little about the subject, people who have a background understanding, or experts? Write a sentence explaining how you can tell.

LANGUAGE AND STRUCTURE

1 Working with a partner, tell her or him about the information you have read in this text. Your partner should make notes about the way you describe the information.

In particular, listen out for:

◆ informal words

◆ longer sentences than are used in the book

◆ fillers (*er, erm*) and repetition – these are known as **non-fluency features**.

2 Like many information texts, this textbook uses quite formal language. It includes some technical words: *perspective, three-dimensional, exploded, interior.*

a Choose one of these technical terms and – using your own words – write down what you think it means.

b Describe something the writer might have done to help a reader who does *not* know that word.

3 Information texts tend to be written mostly in statements. This text includes a question:

Which illustration do you think would be …?

Why do you think the writer includes a question at this point?

4 Look at this sentence:

The following illustration has been drawn using a different exploded drawing method.

a The writer has written this in the passive voice. He or she could have written it in the active voice using the pronoun 'we'. Write an active version of the sentence, starting with 'We'.

b Why do you think the writer chose the passive form?

WRITING ACTIVITY

Imagine a friend has written to you to say that she or he is stuck with Design homework. Write a letter back, explaining about the topic of exploded drawings. Remember to use the present tense, and to use words that give a precise meaning, rather than general description. Use headings and subheadings if you wish.

- How will you structure the information differently?
- How will you address the reader differently?
- How will you use vocabulary and sentences differently?

Write a short paragraph comparing your version with the original.

EXTENDED WRITING

Look at the list of facts below about Florence Nightingale. Your task is to inform Year 7 students about the key facts of her life.

Think about the way you will organize the information.

- How will you use layout features to help the reader?
- What types of sentences will you use (simple, compound, complex)?
- Will you use questions as well as statements?
- Will you use the third person?
- How will you address the reader?
- Will you use the past or present tense?

Florence Nightingale

- Born 1820, died 1910.
- A British hospital reformer and founder of the modern nursing profession.
- She had strong religious convictions.
- She trained as a nurse, and was appointed a nursing superintendent in London in 1853.
- On the outbreak of the Crimean War, in 1854, she volunteered to lead a party of nurses to work in the military hospitals in Scutari, Turkey.
- She set about transforming the appalling conditions. The death rate was reduced from 42% to 2%.
- She earned the nickname 'The Lady with the Lamp'.
- In 1856 she founded Florence Nightingale School and Home for nurses in London.
- She wrote a classic book called *Notes on Nursing*.
- She was awarded the Order of Merit in 1907 – a high award.

You might start by sketching out what your page will look like. You don't need to draw any pictures – just draw a box and write a label saying what the picture would show.

Explanation texts: the essentials

Purpose and audience

Explanation texts explain how things work and why things happen. They give us the answers to questions (such as 'Why did war break out in 1914?') and they are usually clear and direct.

Text level features

Explanation texts will often:

- use **layout features** to make their explanation clearer (e.g. questions, subheadings, boxes, illustrations, diagrams, maps)
- begin with a general **opening statement** ('Europe in 1914 was on the brink of war …')
- give a **step-by-step** account of an event or process
- end with a **summary**.

Sentence level features

Explanation texts usually:

- use the **third-person** form to create an impersonal tone
- use the **present tense** (in science and technical writing, for example) or the **past tense** (for historical writing)
- make some use of the **passive voice** to keep the tone impersonal ('the potassium was then added to the solution')
- use a mix of **simple and compound sentences**
- use **connectives** to show how one idea relates to another and to indicate cause and effect (e.g. *after, until, later*).

Word level features

Explanation texts often use very precise terms, and sometimes **technical language**. This will depend on how much the writer thinks the reader knows about the topic. Explanation text usually avoid using much descriptive language – they will emphasize **facts**. They use nouns and verbs in order to describe processes.

Explaining a process

Why is the sky blue most of the time but can be red at sunset and sunrise?

OBJECTIVES

This website page gives an easy-to-follow explanation of what is happening during a process. These are the objectives you will be studying:

- Word level: *words in context, prepositions and connectives,* and *formality and word choice*

- Sentence level: *tense shifts, conditionals and modal verbs, subject-specific conventions,* and *informal to formal* (identifying the alterations made to change a text from informal to formal)

- Reading: *development of key ideas*

- Writing: *effective information*

Introduction

Most explanation texts answer a question. The text in this unit is taken from the BBC Science Shack website. In it, scientist Adam Hart-Davis answers online questions. To explain science to his audience he uses a mixture of instructions (how to do an experiment) and explanation (showing how the experiment works). He also gives some information about the history of the experiment.

After you have studied this explanation text, you will be able to write one of your own.

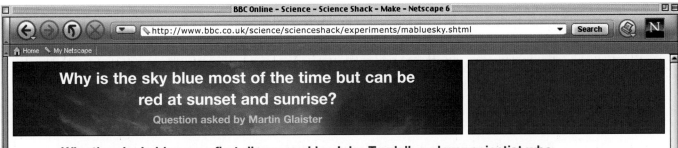

BBC Online – Science – Science Shack – Make – Netscape 6

http://www.bbc.co.uk/science/scienceshack/experiments/mabluesky.shtml

Home   My Netscape

Why is the sky blue most of the time but can be red at sunset and sunrise?

Question asked by Martin Glaister

Why the sky is blue was first discovered by John Tyndall, a clever scientist who succeeded Michael Faraday as director of the Royal Institution in 1867. Tyndall was very good at thinking up demonstrations, and even thought up a way of making his own blue sky. Have a go yourself and see how it works.

What you need:

Fish tank   Torch   Wooden block or books
Dried milk powder   Teaspoon

What to do:

Start by filling the fish tank with water and then balance the torch on the wooden block so that it is shining down the length of the tank. Next add about a quarter teaspoon of milk powder and give it a good stir. Now look at the side of the tank – the water should look slightly blue. This is your sky; it is not very blue, as it is only a very little sky. Look at the end of the fish tank and you should see a yellow sun, your torch. Keep adding milk, a quarter teaspoon at a time, and watch your sky get bluer and your sun turn reddish, like at sunset.

How it works:

Tyndall noticed that when you shone a torch, you could often see the beam. But when he tried this with clean filtered air, he saw nothing at all. He realised that the only reason that you can 'see' beams of light is that the air is full of tiny particles of dust that scatter the light. And this is exactly what is happening in your fish tank. When a ray of light hits a milk particle it bounces off in all directions – the light is scattered. Small particles scatter blue light more than red. This means that when you look at the scattered light from the side of the tank, it is slightly blue, but when you look at the end of the tank you see the rest of the spectrum – mostly yellow and red. So the sky is blue because it is full of tiny floating particles of dust that scatter the blue parts of sunlight. In turn the sun gets redder at sunset as the light travels through more atmosphere, so more light is scattered and only red gets through. Bizarrely, if the air above us were absolutely clear of dust and water, the sky would be black.

Document: Done

Business   Tech   Fun   Interact

UNDERSTANDING THE TEXT

1 Pick out two sentences from the text which you think best answer the reader's question.

2 What was the relationship of John Tyndall to Michael Faraday?

3 What was Tyndall particularly good at?

INTERPRETING THE TEXT

4 How does Adam Hart-Davis use layout to make his explanation easy to follow?

5 How might the writing itself have been made easier to follow? If you had been the editor of the page, would you have added bullet points, shorter paragraphs, more subheadings, words in bold or italics? Write a brief paragraph about how you might make the explanation even clearer.

6 Why do you think Adam Hart-Davis includes historical information about John Tyndall?

7 By the end of the text, do you feel that the original question has been fully answered? Are there any further questions it makes you want to ask?

LANGUAGE AND STRUCTURE

1 Adam Hart-Davis uses a number of sentence functions in his text. Find an example of:

 ◆ a command

 ◆ a statement.

2 a Write down a phrase or sentence in which Adam Hart-Davis uses the past tense.

 b Write down a phrase or sentence in which Adam Hart-Davis uses the present tense.

3 The text is structured like this:

1 introduction
2 ingredients
3 instruction
4 explanation

   a Why is section 1 written mostly in the past tense?

   b Why is the last sentence of this section in the present tense?

   c Why is section 3 in the present tense?

   d Why does section 4 start in the past and then change to the present tense?

4 Look at the instructions in section 3. Write down two connectives the writer uses to show that one instruction follows another.

5 Explanation texts can be written in quite an informal tone. Adam Hart-Davis does this in two main ways.

   a He addresses the reader directly, like this:

   *This means that when **you** look at the scattered light from the side of the tank, it is slightly blue …*

   Write this sentence so that it is more formal and does not refer directly to the reader.

   b He also uses some informal vocabulary, like this:

   *When a ray of light **hits** a milk particle it **bounces off in all directions** …*

   Try to write this in a more formal, technical style, by paying particular attention to the highlighted words.

   c Why do you think Adam Hart-Davis chooses this informal tone?

6 The last section of the text explains how something works. It uses a number of connectives to show how one idea relates to another. Look at the list of connectives below and describe what part each one plays in the text. The first example is done for you.

Connective	Function
And	Shows how this idea continues from the last one
This means	
So	
In turn	
If	

7 Look at the way the writer uses verbs:

Look at the end of the fish tank and you **should** *see a yellow sun …*

How would the effect be different if he had said *you will, might,* or *could* see?

a Which of these modal verbs feels *most* definite?

b Which feels *least* definite?

8 How would you redesign the page to make the process clearer for a younger audience? How would you use images differently? Would you organize the text in a different way?

Map out a new page design for the website. Then write a brief paragraph explaining why your changes would make the information easier for a young reader to understand.

Writing Activity

The extract we have studied here is an explanation of a process that you might explore in a science lesson. How does writing differ in the different subjects you study at school? Use the questions below to reflect on the way you are expected to write. Then put together some writing hints for other students.

a Writing survey

   1 The subject that requires the most writing from me is …

   2 The subject that requires the least writing from me is …

   3 The subject that requires the most formal style is …

   4 The subject that encourages the most detail in my writing is …

   5 The subject that requires the least description is …

b Writing hints

If you were giving advice to a new student on how to produce the best writing in one subject area, what would you say?

Choose one subject and, using these prompts, think of three to five hints you would give for each.

Subject:
Hints on the kinds of words to use (e.g. how technical, how informal, how much description?) ▲ ▲ ▲
Hints on the kinds of sentences (e.g. simple, complex, mostly questions/statements/commands) ▲ ▲ ▲
Hints on how to set out writing (e.g. notes, long paragraphs, bullet-points, subheadings)

Extended Writing

Choose a process you know well. Write an explanation for a general reader. Possible topics might include:

◆ How your school day is organized.

◆ Why people play the national lottery.

◆ How the gears on a bike work.

◆ How a computer spellchecker works.

Make notes of the key points first, then write your explanation, using the third person and the present tense, with connectives to show how one idea relates to another.

What is a media recount?

Introduction

Earlier units in this book looked at several different types of recounts:

- personal recounts ('My First Day at School', page 18)
- newspaper recounts ('Flying Solo', page 44)
- recounts to entertain ('Going Surfing', page 50)
- autobiography (James Herriott, page 58 and Des'ree, page 64).

As you have already learned, recounts:

- may include autobiography, newspaper articles, reports, and historical texts
- aim to inform and entertain
- are usually structured in **chronological order**
- may use the **first person** (autobiography) or the **third person** (history)
- aim to paint pictures in words, so they may use plenty of **description**.

Newspaper recounts

This unit focuses on the types of recounts found in the media, and how they use description.

Newspapers use their front page to inform readers about the stories that seem most important. They then sometimes include further articles on the same topic later in the newspaper, or on a later date. Here the purpose might be to provide more detailed information or different viewpoints. Our first extract is of this type.

Newspapers also investigate events that are not major news – mysteries, amusing stories, or local events. The second extract in this unit is an example of this type of article.

News article

An Ealing Comedy of Errors

> ### OBJECTIVES
>
> This extract gives newspaper readers the facts about a news event. These are the objectives you will be studying:
>
> - Word level: *layers of meaning*
> - Sentence level: *degrees of formality, integrate speech, reference and quotation,* and *paragraph organization*
> - Reading: *evaluate information, readers and texts* (how they influence each other), *author's standpoint,* and *rhetorical devices*
> - Writing: *'infotainment'* (how information texts can be amusing and entertaining), and *descriptive detail*

Introduction

This extract gives the 'inside story' about a daring raid at the Millennium Dome in Greenwich, on 7 November 2000. Readers will probably have read the main story, which was on pages 1 and 2 of the newspaper. This article aims to give more detailed information, using language and images to help explain what happened.

> ### GLOSSARY
>
> **Ealing Comedy** – *early British comedy films which were made at studios in Ealing*

AN EALING COMEDY OF ERRORS

By Bill Mouland and Stephen Wright

After months of meticulous planning, the raiders must have thought nothing could stop them

A boat was waiting to whisk the gang away. So were the police.

It was like a scene from The Sweeney as the gang's stolen JCB smashed into the Dome and roared towards its multi-million target.

With a speedboat idling its powerful engines on the Thames outside and a lookout monitoring police radio frequencies on the opposite bank, the thieves must have thought nothing could stop them.

But a gritty drama of criminal daring swiftly turned into something more akin to an Ealing comedy. For police had known about the plot for two months and 100 officers were lying in wait – some disguised as cleaners, others as tourists.

Staff from De Beers, which owns the Millennium Star and the other 11 rare blue diamonds in the spectacular Money Zone display, were also in on the act and had already swapped the real gems for fakes.

The police watched and waited as four of the gang, all wearing gas masks and bulletproof vests, let off smoke bombs and thunder flashes in the vault.

They were starting to attack the display with nail guns and sledgehammers when the Flying Squad, the real-life Sweeney, went into action.

Shouting 'Stop! Armed police,' about 20 officers surrounded the gang while snipers held them in their sights from overhead gantries.

They gave up without a fight, visibly shocked that they had walked straight into a trap.

Flying Squad chief Detective Superintendent Jon Shatford, who led the operation, said 'They were absolutely startled. They were facing armed officers with guns pointed at them. I don't think they were too happy about that.'

Outside, other officers grabbed the drivers of the getaway boat and lookout van.

Last night Scotland Yard said 12 people in all had been arrested, including alleged accomplices held at addresses in Kent and London.

The astonishing raid attempt could easily have been inspired by the latest James Bond blockbuster The World is not Enough, in which the Dome is the backdrop for a dramatic chase sequence involving speedboats.

'Audacious response'

One of the film's stars, Sophie Marceau, was also pictured last year clutching the Millennium Star Diamond, the jewel which played a focal part in the Millennium Eve celebrations when laser beams were fired through its many facets.

Makers Metro Goldwyn Mayer were quick to use the raid to publicise the film. But Mr Shatford refused to be carried away by the hype, saying: 'There has been lots of talk about James Bond but I don't want to glamorise anything the gang has done.

'It was an audacious robbery which could have terrorised members of the public. Fortunately it was foiled by a more audacious police response.'

The drama began at daybreak when police involved in the operation – codename: Magician – began to take up their positions, just as they had done a number of times in the past few weeks.

Those had been false alarms, this time it was for real.

More than 60 members of the public, including schoolchildren rehearsing for a show, were already in the Dome when the arrival of the getaway boat and the lookout van signalled that the raid was about to take place.

The visitors were led to safety by staff who had also been briefed by police. Some were taken to the on site McDonald's restaurant, others to see a Blackadder video.

Within minutes, at 9.30am, the four men aboard the stolen JCB had crashed through the perimeter and Operation Magician was in full swing. The Dome was sealed off and a 100 metre exclusion zone was being set up even as the digger plunged through the plexiglass door, drove past the Learning and Work zones and rammed the entrance to the Millennium Jewels exhibit.

One eye witness said: 'I heard this enormous crashing noise. My first thought was that something had fallen on top of the Dome – it was so loud. But then I saw this JCB moving towards the Money Zone. I could see two men on it, one driving and the other clinging to the side.'

Café manager Ozcan Ocak said: 'When the JCB came through the wall there was a massive crashing sound. The next thing I knew there was smoke everywhere and the police were running towards it from all directions.

'I saw one police officer, disguised as a cleaner, pulling a gun from a bin bag. It looked like a machine-gun. The police were very heavily armed.'

He added: 'It was very frightening for my customers because some police officers came running towards me screaming, "Get down, get down". Some customers, including an elderly lady, were forced to crouch behind our counter while others hid under tables and behind the staircase next to our café.

'Nobody really knew what was going on, in fact I'm convinced some people thought it was a Millennium Dome stunt.

'When I saw the guns I knew it was very real indeed, I've never felt so frightened in my life.'

Among the visitors were 64 pupils aged 11 to 16 from 23 schools in Dorset. They were there to perform in a show called Our Town.

Project assistant Mandy Sylvester said: 'It was very scary. We were just setting up the exhibition profiling Dorset and the show outside the McDonald's Theatre when we were shouted at to "get into the theatre now!"

'I saw a policeman next to me with a gun. The next thing, I heard gunfire and helicopters and everyone in the theatre was terrified.'

While the police faced criticism for allowing children to be exposed to possible danger, they received full backing from both the Dome management and Dorset education officials.

Dome executive chairman David James, said: 'Our concern was the safety of our visitors and the people who work at The Dome. Steps were taken throughout to ensure that our visitors were not put at risk.'

UNDERSTANDING THE TEXT

1 For how long had police known about the plot?

2 How many people were arrested?

3 How many members of the public were in the Dome when the raid began?

4 Using the whole article, write a topic sentence which explains to a new reader what happened at the Dome on 7 November 2000.

INTERPRETING THE TEXT

5 Quite a lot of readers may not understand the headline if they do not know about Ealing comedies.

   a Why do you think the editor of this page wants to compare the robbery to comedy films?

   b What does this tell you about the audience the newspaper is aimed at?

> ## HINTS
>
> - Ealing comedies were made in the 1940s and 1950s
> - They are well known to people of all ages who are interested in the history of films

6 Look at the way the robbers are presented in the article. Are they shown as:

daring   foolish   dangerous   unlucky?

Choose one or two words that best sum up the way the article presents them. Find some examples from the article to support your choices.

7 Newspaper reports often blend fact with opinion. Look at this sentence from the article:

But a gritty drama of criminal daring swiftly turned into something more akin to an Ealing comedy.

How far is this sentence fact and how far is it opinion? Can you tell the writer's attitude from it? If you were to write the information in a purely factual sentence, how would you express it?

8 The writers describe it as 'the astonishing raid attempt'. Why do you think they include the word 'astonishing'?

9 Some readers may feel that the article contains quite a lot of the authors' own opinions, and also that it makes the raid seem glamorous. Do you agree?

HINTS

- Find some examples first of where the writers use words to suggest their own opinions

- Then say whether you think they make the raid seem glamorous

LANGUAGE AND STRUCTURE

1 We normally expect the first paragraph of a newspaper article to use a topic sentence – a sentence that tells us the whole story (answering the questions *who, what, where, when?*).

a How is this paragraph different from what we might expect?

b How does the writer try to grab our attention with this opening? Do you think it works?

2 The structure of the article is:

- first describe the raid

- then give quotations from eyewitnesses.

a Why does the writer include quotations from eyewitnesses? How would the story be different without them?

b Look at these statements by witnesses:

   i *I heard this enormous crashing noise* (eyewitness)

   ii *It was very scary* (Mandy Sylvester)

   iii *Our concern was the safety of our visitors and the people who work at The Dome* (David James)

Which of these statements:

◆ feels most informal? How can you tell?

◆ feels most formal? How can you tell?

3 David James says:

Steps were taken throughout to ensure that our visitors were not put at risk.

This uses the passive voice ('Steps were taken').

a How could the same idea have been expressed using the active voice, starting like this: 'We . . .'

b What difference does using the passive voice make?

WRITING ACTIVITY

Think about why newspaper recounts use quotations from different people involved in a story. Imagine you were covering the story of an attempted burglary at your school. A gang tried to steal 25 computers, but they were foiled by the school caretaker.

Apart from recounting what happened, who would you want quotations from? Remember that newspapers like to use several different points of view where possible.

When you have decided who your quotations would come from, make up the words these people would say. The quotations need to be brief and to the point. Try to make them sound like real spoken statements.

Newspaper investigation

The Lancashire Cat Mystery

OBJECTIVES

This extract treats an unusual event in an original way. You will be studying these objectives:

- Word level: *connectives for developing thought*

- Sentence level: *degrees of formality, integrate speech, reference and quotation,* and *paragraph organization*

- Reading: *evaluate information, readers and texts* (how they influence each other), *author's standpoint,* and *rhetorical devices*

- Writing: *creativity in non-literary texts, 'infotainment'* (how information texts can be amusing and entertaining), and *descriptive detail*

Introduction

This article reports an event that would probably not be put on the front pages of most national newspapers. Yet it is causing deep concern in a Lancashire village. As you read it, look in particular at the sources of the story – the main people who are quoted and what they say. Decide how reliable you think the whole story is. When you have finished studying this article, you can write one of your own.

In a little Lancashire village, a cat a day is vanishing into thin air. What is going on?

By Ian Herbert, Northern Correspondent

The rumour spread like wildfire through the east Lancashire village of Lumb yesterday. Fourteen cats, so the whisper went, had been seen dead in an isolated country lane. The details were precise, police officers searched, but by nightfall their efforts had come to nothing.

This means the village is still no nearer an explanation to a baffling riddle that is fuelling rumour and counter-rumour. Fifteen cats have vanished here in the space of two weeks from an area of just a few hundred square yards, but no one knows why.

There is an abundance of theories and, in the words of PC Bill King, the neighbourhood officer, 'none of them are pleasant'. The creatures have been taken for the fur trade, say some. A cat killer is on the loose, claim others. There is even a suggestion that the cats have been sold to research laboratories.

Whatever the answer, the saga has left locals living on frayed nerves and the village postmaster's door plastered with photographs of lamented pets. 'We've lost our Chloe, a timid, ginger she-cat,' reads one, between posters for Lumb Baptist Church's football night and a holy beetle drive. 'Missing cat, if seen please telephone,' says another. 'Fluffy, green eyes, very nervous, £200 for safe return.'

The first to vanish from the village, in the Rossendale Valley between Rawtenstall and Burnley, were three rare pedigree Bengals. Two of them, blue-eyed Emma and Ella, were the first snow leopard variety ever bred in Britain and worth £1,250. When they went missing on 2 November, many people believed they had been stolen because of their value.

Their owner, Lisa Shasby, also lost a six-year-old ginger called Axl a week later, though, and it then seemed the cats were being picked off indiscriminately. The Parkinson family on a neighbouring street lost their two-week-old ginger, Jasper, a week ago. 'Three went on the worst single night,' said PC King.

His own search has taken him through the bed of the nearby Whitewell brook while locals have combed fields in the valley. To have found a dead or injured cat would have been a blessing in some ways, said PC King, who is based at nearby Bacup. 'It is the lack of tangible evidence of these cats which makes us believe something sinister is going on. There's more to this than just "cats will be cats",' he said.

PC King discounts a few more far-fetched explanations. Fifteen years ago, for instance, it was said the Beast of Rossendale roamed these parts. 'There's no danger of that,' said PC King. 'The *Daily Star* also interviewed someone who claimed the "Beast of Bacup ate my Butties" a few years ago but all that's nonsense.'

The charity Pet Search UK said it has never known so many cats go in such a small area though these incidents do follow a case in the Huddersfield suburb of Marsh last month, in which 25 cats fell victim to a poisoner.

In Lumb, 27-year-old Mrs Shasby has just one cat left, a Bengal called Taz. 'I am not letting him out of my sight. He is barricaded inside,' she said.

Last night, as a Lancashire Police spokeswoman confirmed the cats were 'still not accounted for', PC King sent a message to anyone who might try to take a 16th. 'If this person thinks he can come to Lancashire and steal cats he should think again,' he said. 'If he comes back here I'll have him.'

UNDERSTANDING THE TEXT

1 What is the name of the village where the incidents are taking place?

2 How many cats have disappeared so far?

3 What three different theories are there about where the cats are disappearing to?

4 What was the first case of cats disappearing?

5 How many cats disappeared on the worst night?

INTERPRETING THE TEXT

6 Not all newspaper articles are meant to be taken entirely seriously. As you read this article, did you feel that it was a serious news story? Explain your answer.

7 We expect newspaper headings to be short and punchy. This one is not. Unusually, it uses two sentences.

   a What is the headline writer aiming to achieve?

   b How well do you think it works?

   c Think of a headline in a more conventional style.

8 If this were a front page news article, we would expect it to begin with a topic sentence summarizing the whole story.

   a Why do you think it does not do that?

   b Write a topic sentence which would work as a summary.

9 What can you tell about the writer's attitude to the events? Can you tell anything also about his attitude to his readers (e.g. does he know the kind of story they like, does he aim chiefly to entertain rather than inform them)?

Choose a statement from those below which best sums up what we can say about the writer's attitude. Then write a sentence explaining your choice.

   a It is impossible to tell what the writer's attitude is.

   b The writer is genuinely concerned.

   c The writer treats it as something of a joke.

10 How does the writer make readers want to keep reading on? You might mention:

   ◆ the headline

   ◆ the opening paragraph

   ◆ the way he builds tension

   ◆ the quotations he includes.

LANGUAGE AND STRUCTURE

1 Look again at the opening sentence where the author uses a rhetorical device to hook our interest: he might have begun with the phrase '*A rumour*', but instead he writes '*The rumour*'. What is the effect of using the definite article '*the*'?

2 Look at PC King's language. It is quite formal and complex.

> *It is the lack of tangible evidence of these cats which makes us believe something sinister is going on.*

a Why do you think PC King speaks in this formal way? Think about how his language contrasts with that of the other residents.

b If he were just chatting to someone more informally, how do you think the policeman might have expressed the same ideas in a more informal way?

3 Recounts tell us about events in a chronological sequence. They link sentences and paragraphs together with connectives to show one event developing out of another. Write down two or three connectives you notice the writer using.

WRITING ACTIVITY

Look back to the Writing Activity on page 93. It explored the quotations you might include in a story about a bungled burglary at your school.

Now write the opening of the burglary story, in the way that this newspaper journalist writes about the Lancashire cat mystery. Think of ways to portray the burglars as foolish. Give your school caretaker a very formal style of speech, like PC King. Aim to entertain your readers with a lively recount. You might start with a joke like this:

They thought they'd leave with PCs. Instead the PCs left with them.

or with a dramatic statement like this:

An unusually quiet night for school caretaker Fred Smith was suddenly shattered when ...

EXTENDED WRITING

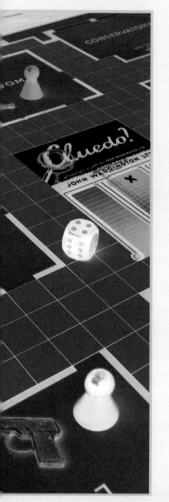

Create your own recount about a crime for a national newspaper. Use quotations from different eyewitnesses to make it entertaining as well as informative.

You could choose to base your story on the game of Cluedo. Imagine that a murder attempt has taken place in a large old house. A detective arrives and finds a host of unlikely characters:

♦ Reverend Green

♦ Miss Scarlet

♦ Professor Plum

♦ Mrs White

♦ Colonel Mustard

The murder attempt took place in the kitchen with a revolver. The assassin missed her or his target but did not manage to escape from the house. The detective interviewed all the suspects before realizing it was just a game.

The newspaper editor wants you to make this into an entertaining story, with wacky characters and an inefficient police officer.

♦ Think of how you will start your article – the aim will be to make it entertaining, so that readers realize it is a jokey piece.

♦ Think of quotations from the different people involved, including your detective.

♦ Think of how you will structure your article so that you can retell the events of the night.

You could begin like this …

Perhaps the police need to spend a little more time playing board games.

A gunshot was overheard by neighbours at Bagshott Manor in the early hours of yesterday morning. They immediately dialled 999 …

Set out your story as a newspaper article, showing how you would lay out the text, and where you would use a larger text size, bullet points or illustrations.

Travel writing: the essentials

Introduction

Travel writing shows us people and places through the eyes of the writer. Often the setting is exotic – for example, Bill Bryson describes going surfing in Australia. Writers might also describe places nearer to home – for example, another famous traveller, Eric Newby, described the exciting memories he had of travelling through Harrods, the London department store.

Travel writing:

◆ reports on the experiences of going to places and meeting people

◆ may aim to inform as well as entertain us

◆ is usually retold in **chronological order**

◆ usually uses the **first person**

◆ aims to paint pictures in words, so it may use plenty of **descriptive language**.

Dramatic travel recount
Sinking Fast

OBJECTIVES

This extract is a very dramatic and entertaining recount of an incident that took place on a journey. You will be studying the following objectives:

- Word level: *terminology for analysis* (using appropriate terms for analysing language) and *layers of meaning*

- Sentence level: *complex sentences*, and *punctuation for clarity and effect*

- Reading: *rhetorical devices*

- Writing: *'infotainment'* (how information texts can be amusing and entertaining), *integrate information*, and *descriptive detail*

Introduction

This text shows how recounts can be dramatic and full of impact. Steve Callahan is an American yachtsman. In this extract from his book *Adrift*, he is sailing single-handed between England and Antigua in his yacht, 'Napoleon Solo'. When you have studied this dramatic recount, you can try writing one of your own.

GLOSSARY

tumultuous – *stormy*

pile driver – *a machine for driving beams of wood, metal or concrete into the ground*

buccaneer – *pirate*

aft pulpit – *a raised, railed-in area at the back of a yacht, from which the sailor has a clear view*

SINKING FAST.

It is about 22:30 Greenwich Mean Time. The moon hangs full, white and motionless, undisturbed by the tempest and the tumultuous sea. If conditions continue to worsen, I will have to head more southerly. For the time being, I can do nothing more, so I lie down to rest. At 23:00 I get up and undress. I lie down again clothed only in a T-shirt. A watch circles my wrist, and around my neck is a slab of whale tooth on a string. It is the most I will wear the next two and a half months.

My boat slews around the rushing peaks, her keel clinging to the slopes like a mountain goat, her port side pressed down against the black, rolling ocean. I lie on my bunk, slung upon the lee canvas, hanging as if in a hammock.

BANG! A deafening explosion blankets the subtler sounds of torn wood fibre and rush of sea. I jump up. Water thunders over me as if I've suddenly been thrown into the path of a rampaging river. Forward, aft – where does it come from? Is half of the side gone? No time. I fumble with the knife I have sheathed by the chart table. Already the water is waist deep. The nose of the boat is dipping down. *Solo* comes to a halt as she begins a sickening dive. She's going down, down! My mind barks orders. Free the emergency package. My soul screams. You've lost her! I hold my breath, submerge, slash at the tie-downs that secure my emergency duffel. My heart is a pounding pile driver. The heavy work wrings the air from my lungs and my mind battles with my limbs for the opportunity to breathe. Terminal darkness and chaos surround me. Get out, get out, she's going down! In one rhythmic movement I rocket upward, thrust the hatch forward, and catapult my shaking body on to the deck, leaving my package of hope behind.

Less than thirty seconds have elapsed since impact. The bow points toward its grave at a hesitating low angle and the sea washes about my ankles. I cut the tie-downs that secure the raft canister. Thoughts flash about me like echoes in a cave. Perhaps I have waited too long. Perhaps it is time to die. Going down… die … lost without trace. I recall the life raft instructions: throw the bulky hundred pounds overboard before inflation. Who can manoeuvre such weight in the middle of a bucking circus ride? No time, quickly – she's going down! I yank. The first pull, then the second – nothing, nothing! This is it, the end of my life. Soon, it will come soon. I scream at the stubborn canister. The third pull comes up hard, and she blows with a bursting static *shush*. A wave sweeps over the entire deck, and I simply float the raft off. It thrashes about on the end of its painter. *Solo* has been transformed from a proper little ship to a submerged wreck in about one minute. I dive into the raft with the knife clenched in my teeth, buccaneer style, noticing that the movie camera mounted on the aft pulpit has been turned on. Its red eye winks at me. Who is directing this film? He isn't much on lighting but his flair for the dramatic is impressive.

Unmoving and unconcerned, the moon looks down upon us. Its lunar face is eclipsed by wisps of clouds that waft across it, dimming the shadow of *Solo's* death. My instincts and training have carried me through the motions of survival, but now, as I have a moment to reflect, the full impact of the crash throbs in my head. Never have all of my senses seemed so sharp. My emotions are an incomprehensible mix. There is a wailing anguish that mourns the loss of my boat. There is a deep disappointment in myself for my failures. Overshadowing it all is the stark realization that what I think and feel will not matter much longer. My body shakes with cold. I am too far from civilization to have any hope of rescue.

UNDERSTANDING THE TEXT

1 How would you describe the weather conditions Steve Callahan is facing?

2 Explain what you think the writer means by 'my heart is a pounding pile driver'.

3 Write down two of the emotions Steve Callahan feels towards the end of the extract.

INTERPRETING THE TEXT

4 How does the writer make the yacht seem as if it's alive? Look in particular at the language he uses in the second paragraph.

5 Look at paragraph 3 in more detail.

   a How does Steve Callahan use words to recreate the drama of this experience at sea? Look at:

- his use of vocabulary
- ways in which he helps the reader to visualize the scene.

   b Look at the way he uses sentences to create impact. What do you notice about:

- his use of very short and much longer sentences? Why does he do this?
- his mix of statements and questions? What effect does this have?

   Write a short paragraph about this.

6 a Look at this sentence:

Unmoving and unconcerned, the moon looks down upon us.

How is the writer presenting the moon here?

> **HINT**
>
> Look at the use of the verb 'looks down'

b The writer also uses other rhetorical devices, such as metaphors. Find an example of a metaphor that you think is particularly effective.

7 What picture do you get of Steve Callahan from the extract? Does he seem:

calm   disappointed   angry   aggressive   shocked   uncontrolled

Choose the word that you think best fits him, and then write a sentence or two explaining why you have chosen it.

LANGUAGE AND STRUCTURE

1 Writers use various devices to make their accounts dramatic. Look at this writer's use of punctuation in paragraph 3. Notice how he uses:

 ◆ capital letters

 ◆ exclamation marks

 ◆ dashes.

How do all of these increase the sense of drama?

2 The writer uses some very short sentences: 'My soul screams.' 'I yank.' These are used alongside some much longer sentences. What effect would it create if he used:

a abrupt, short sentences all the time?

b longer, more complex sentences all the time?

3 The writer uses vivid language to show us the thoughts going through his mind. Look at the way he uses active verbs to increase the drama:

 ◆ my mind **barks** orders

 ◆ the heavy work **wrings** the air from my lungs

 ◆ my mind **battles** with my limbs

 ◆ I **rocket** upward.

a For each of these, think of a different verb the writer might have used (e.g. 'move' instead of 'rocket').

b Describe the different effect of the new word (e.g. 'move' does not have the same sense of speed or rapid movement as 'rocket').

4 Steve Callahan writes a dramatic and often emotional account of being caught in a storm. What would a more factual, less emotional version sound like? Take the main events in the text and write them down in a three-paragraph report, using this frame:

1 Say what we know about the yachtsman.

2 Describe the weather.

3 Describe what happens.

WRITING ACTIVITY

Write about a dramatic moment in your own life, using some of the techniques Steve Callahan uses, such as:

♦ active verbs

♦ abrupt, dramatic, short sentences

♦ onomatopoeic words (e.g. 'bang', 'shush').

Try to show a) what happened and b) the thoughts that raced through your mind.

Your chosen topics might include:

♦ a time you were involved in an accident

♦ a time you were terrified of being at a height

♦ a theme park ride that filled you with terror.

To give your recount maximum impact, aim to use:

♦ a mix of short and longer sentences

♦ vivid visual details

♦ clear description of your own thoughts at the time

♦ appropriate punctuation, including occasional dashes, capital letters and exclamation marks.

Descriptive travel recount

A Desert Dies

OBJECTIVES

This extract gives a highly descriptive recount of the traveller's experiences. These are the objectives you will study:

- Word level: *layers of meaning*
- Sentence level: *degrees of formality*
- Reading: *note-making at speed*, and *rhetorical devices*
- Writing: *creativity in non-literary texts*, and *integrate information*

Introduction

In 1985, teacher Michael Asher joined a tribe of desert nomads as they travelled across the Sahara seeking food and shelter. The vast Sahara desert is dying, becoming a waste land, and its people are being forced out.

Like all the best travel writing, Michael Asher's recount gives us personal opinion mixed with strong, vivid description. This extract describes a desert storm. When you have studied the piece, you will be able to write a vivid recount of one of your own journeys.

GLOSSARY

Wadi – *a riverbed which is dry except in the rainy season*

Ochre – *a yellow brown colour*

Hobbles - *fastenings put on an animal's legs to limit its movement*

Quagmire - *bog*

Morass - *bog*

A Desert Dies . . . .

I was woken by a clap of thunder that shook the air like an explosion. Streaks of lightning forked down to the earth, and a second later rain came surging out of the night sky, spattering across the dust in enormous droplets. Within minutes the wadi was inches deep in water, and before we could move it

was up to our calves. Still heavy with sleep, we tried desperately to shift our gear, but the water rose second by second. 'Hold on to your things!' someone shouted. The water was pouring into the wash from all sides, and for a moment I wondered if we might drown. I stayed where I was, and held on grimly to my saddle-bags, praying that my camera and film would survive. Soon the water was up to my thighs, and I crouched there, trying to keep my balance as the soft sand under my feet began to melt away. I had often heard of Arabs being drowned in wadis by flash floods, and had found it difficult to believe that the water-level could rise so rapidly. I tensed my muscles and stayed without shifting for what seemed like hours as the rain slopped down the back of my shirt. Pieces of twig and tufts of grass nudged against me as they floated downstream in the torrent. I hardly noticed the rain easing off, until it had become no more than a light drizzle. Gradually the water began to subside. By morning it had disappeared completely.

The sickly grey light of dawn crept over the world to reveal a landscape transformed. Everywhere the thorn trees glinted and dripped with moisture, and the grey dust had turned into a rippled carpet of ochre mud that was plastered over the tree trunks. Masses of woody debris and uprooted bushes were piled up along the sides of the wadi. Some of the camels had been half buried in the slime, unable to move because of their hobbles. They sat there, uncomplaining, silently waiting to be released. Many of my things had been carried away. I had lost my sandals, whip, pipe, books and saddle-cushions. My camera and lenses were full of muddy water and most of my film was wet. My maps looked like papier mâché and my tobacco was a pulpy mess. I watched my companions dragging

their gear out of the mud, looking miserable and bedraggled. It was an irony that when rain fell in this thirsty land, it almost always brought greater hardship. None of us was in any mood to celebrate. Wad az Zayadi announced that the flour was soaked and the seasoning ruined. All our leather equipment was waterlogged and our saddles splattered with mud.

'Come on, let's pull the camels out!' At Tom said, and we went to inspect the animals. Some of them were stuck tight, where the wadi floor had melted under their weight. We had to go down on our hands and knees in the slime to unfasten their hobbles, then slither about trying to fix their headropes. In places the mud was up to our calves, and we slipped and staggered as we tried to heave the animals out of the quagmire. I hauled on Wad al 'Atiga's rope as Hamid pushed him from the rear. The beast roared and whined in confusion, and suddenly jerked back on the rope so that I plummeted into the mud-slick. Hamid began to laugh uproariously, until he too lost his footing and was sitting up to his waist in the ooze. After that he gave up and started to crawl out of the morass on his hands and knees. It took us more than an hour to drag the slime-sodden animals on to drier ground. They looked a sorry sight, their buff hide covered in slicks of red muck. Afterwards we laid our sheepskins and blankets out to dry, and Wad az Zayadi emptied the flour and seasoning on to plastic sheets. Then we began to hunt for our lost possessions. Most of them were found stuck between the split roots of bushes or covered in mud on the wadi-bed. After another hour I had found all but my pipe. I had begun to despair, when Wad Fadul held it up, grinning. I knocked a pellet of muck out of its bowl and found that it was still smokable.

UNDERSTANDING THE TEXT

1 What surprises the writer about the storm?

2 What is the writer most anxious to save from the flood?

3 How has the storm affected some of the camels?

4 Name two other effects the storm has.

INTERPRETING THE TEXT

5 Look more closely at the first paragraph. How can you tell that the writer really feels afraid of the storm? Pick out the sentence which you think best shows this.

6 What impression do you get of the writer from the text? Write a short paragraph about your response to him. Choose some of the words below if you feel they are appropriate. In your paragraph, aim to support each point with an example.

WORD BANK

Afraid, nervous, apprehensive, cowardly, terrified, bold, courageous, determined, thoughtful, angry, dismayed, worried, bitter, disappointed, confused, concerned for others, compassionate, selfish, patient

7 What picture do you normally have of the landscape of a desert? In what ways does the picture presented in this text differ from that?

8 a What impression do you get of Michael Asher's relationship with the tribes-people? How does he get on with them?

　b What impression do you get of his attitude to the camels?

LANGUAGE AND STRUCTURE

1 One way writers can make descriptions vivid is by using dramatic language. Look at Michael Asher's description of the storm:

*I was woken by a clap of thunder that **shook** the air like an explosion. Streaks of lightning **forked** down to the earth, and a second later rain came **surging** out of the night sky, **spattering** across the dust in enormous droplets.*

Look at the four highlighted verbs. For each one, look at the different word listed below, that the writer might have used:

Shook – sounded in
Forked – came
Surging – falling
Spattering – dropping

  a Compare the two sets of verbs. Why does Michael Asher's choice of verbs make the storm seem so much more dramatic?

  b Michael Asher also uses a simile:

    *A clap of thunder that shook the air **like an explosion***

    What impression of the thunder does the noun 'explosion' create?

2 Travel writers sometimes use words from the culture they are visiting. Michael Asher uses Arabic words throughout his writing. In this extract he uses the word *wadi*, meaning 'dry river bed'. Some writers might have used the English phrase instead. Why do you think he chooses to use the Arabic term?

3 Look at the start of paragraph 2:

The sickly grey light of dawn crept over the world ...

Some writers might have written: 'Dawn was grey ...'. What picture of the dawn does the writer's image create?

4 Look at the way the writer describes the scene:

Everywhere the thorn trees glinted and dripped with moisture, and the grey dust had turned into a rippled carpet of ochre mud that was plastered over the tree trunks.

This sentence is rich in description. How might you write it in a less descriptive way, so that it communicated only facts?

5 Look at the range of sentences the writer uses in this second paragraph.

- Some of them are chiefly description.
- Some say what happened next.
- Some express an opinion.

Find a sentence that fits each of these functions.

WRITING ACTIVITY

Michael Asher's recount is highly descriptive, helping us to visualize the desert scene, the storm, and the effect it has on the people and camels.

How would a purely factual account of his experiences be different? Imagine that you have been asked to list the events that take place in the extract, but not to give much description.

Re-read the text and quickly take down some notes about what happens. Then write a formal recount which simply retells the events. You will probably be able to do this in one paragraph.

Now write a few sentences describing the way you approached this task:

- what you were looking for as you took your notes
- the main parts of the original text that had to be left out
- how you knew which parts of the text to keep
- how you made your tone factual.

EXTENDED WRITING

The description given in recounts helps a reader to see, hear and smell the scene that is being described. This is especially important in travel writing, which aims to create a vivid picture.

Think of a journey you have taken. It does not need to be exotic – it might be quite an ordinary journey, like these:

◆ your journey to school

◆ a journey around a supermarket

◆ a journey to a friend's house.

Your challenge is to bring that journey alive for the reader. Use vivid, descriptive writing to recreate the journey in words. You do not need to write a long piece of work; instead, the emphasis is on very concentrated writing.

Think about the following points:

1 Avoid using the first person all the time ('I noticed the rough road' becomes 'the road is rough and badly mended').

2 Combine description, plot and opinion.

◆ Description: 'The bike had rusted slightly, and whatever paint had first been applied had now faded into a strange orange grime.'

◆ Plot: 'I turned the corner, expecting to see box after box of breakfast cereal, but instead …'

◆ Opinion: 'Every visit to the supermarket leaves me feeling worried – have I spent too much? Have I forgotten something? Was that the right bacon?'

3 Create vivid description by using active verbs (*exploded, surging, spattering*), adjectives and adverbs, sensuous words (describing sights, sounds, textures, tastes, smells) and similes (' … shook the air like an explosion').

As a starting-point, you might begin your account by describing how you closed the door behind you, like this …

I slammed the door behind me. My journey had begun …

How information texts work

12

Introduction

So far we have looked at several information texts:

- Young Citizen's Passport (page 2)
- A Guide to Health (page 6)
- Exploded Drawings (page 72)

This unit focuses on the way information texts can also combine elements of instruction and persuasion. They will be giving you information, but this is then used as a source of advice.

Information texts describe how things are. They are written for an audience who will usually want to know more about the topic, but may already have some knowledge of the subject.

Information texts will be clear, well-ordered, and easy to follow, often using **layout features** such as tables and diagrams to help make the information clear. They usually place information in **order of importance**, not chronological order.

Usually they use the **third-person** form to create an impersonal tone, and the **present tense**. Often they use very precise terms, and sometimes **technical language**. The level of technical language will depend on how much the writer thinks the reader already knows about the topic.

Information texts avoid using much descriptive language. They will emphasize **facts**.

Informing and persuading

Choosing to Be Vegetarian

> ### Objectives
>
> Here we compare two examples of information texts that intend to persuade their audience to do something: a leaflet and a web page. You will be studying the following objectives:
>
> - Word level: *apply knowledge* (of word origins), and *connectives for developing thought*
> - Sentence level: *paragraph organization*, and *conventions of ICT texts*
> - Reading: *synthesize information* (put it together from different sources), *evaluate information, compare texts*, and *author's standpoint*
> - Writing: *presentational devices, integrate information, explain connections*, and *effective presentation of information*

Introduction

Leaflets are an important way of giving information. A simple leaflet may be a sheet of printed paper, folded in half. More sophisticated leaflets use text and graphics to clarify ideas and, in some cases, to persuade the reader to change his or her opinion or to buy a specific product.

Websites are also an important way of presenting information. As with leaflets, they can use a range of design features to help get their information across to the reader – including interactive techniques and animations.

These two texts are on the subject of vegetarianism. The first is a Sainsbury's leaflet. It aims to inform customers about vegetarian options. The second text is from the Vegetarian Society website. It is about the ways vegetarianism helps animals and the environment.

Both texts aim to do more than just inform us. They both also have persuasive purposes. When you have studied the two texts, you will create a poster that aims to inform and persuade.

Text A

a **vegetarian** choice

Almost 7 million people in the UK are now vegetarian, or have cut down to eating meat just once or twice a week. A vegetarian lifestyle is more popular than ever, with an estimated 5,000 people deciding to become vegetarian every week.

An interest in food and health, concerns over animal welfare, and concerns about the environment, are three reasons some people give for choosing a vegetarian diet.

A vegetarian diet can provide all the nutrients and energy you need provided you get the right balance of foods. A healthy vegetarian diet contains plenty of fruit and vegetables, starchy foods like bread and pasta, dairy products and alternatives to meat such as pulses (peas, beans, lentils).

'Vegetarianism' isn't just for those who have given up meat, poultry and fish altogether. Every day people in the UK buy meatfree products or choose the vegetarian option on a menu simply because they enjoy the taste. A vegetarian choice is one that anyone can make.

healthy eating made easy

When shopping at Sainsbury's for a healthy vegetarian diet our clear labelling will help you make quick decisions about the foods that are right for you.

'Suitable for vegetarians' symbol

Sainsbury's vegetarian symbol appears on about 1000 products that are suitable for lacto-ovo vegetarians. It is generally used on products that vegetarians might not know are suitable. It is not used on foods that are obviously suitable for vegetarians, such as fruit and vegetables.

what is a vegetarian?

A vegetarian does not eat meat, poultry or fish, and also avoids animal by-products like gelatine (a thickening ingredient in foods, made from animal bones).

there are different groups of vegetarians

- **lacto-ovo vegetarians** make up the majority of vegetarians. They eat dairy products and eggs. Some vegetarians choose to only eat eggs that are free range.

- **lacto-vegetarians** are those who avoid eggs.

- **vegans** are vegetarians who consume no animal products at all.

- **demi-vegetarians** are a relatively new group. These are people who don't eat red meat but still eat white meat or fish occasionally.

'Healthy Balance Symbol'

The Sainsbury's Healthy Balance symbol is an easy way to help you eat more healthily. Foods carrying this symbol have a limited amount of fat, particularly saturated fat, and also have limited amounts of added sugar and sodium (salt).

Around 2,000 products now carry the symbol, so it should be easier to make healthier choices. The symbol also appears on a few foods that are high in fat, such as vegetable oils and spreads, the symbol highlights the healthier option.

Nutritional labelling

Most of our own label products carry full nutritional labelling.

We give information per serving and per 100g, on the food once it has been prepared or cooked according to the instructions.

NUTRITION INFORMATION		
TYPICAL VALUES (cooked as per instructions)		
	per FLAN	per 100g
ENERGY	1462 kj	975kj
	351 k cal	234 k cal
PROTEIN	9.0g	6.0g
CARBOHYDRATE	28.2g	18.8g
of which sugars	3.0g	2.0g
of which starch	25.2g	16.8g
FAT	22.3g	14.9g
of which saturates	7.6g	5.1g
of which mono-unsaturates	10.9g	7.3g
of which polysaturates	2.7g	1.8g
FIBRE	1.6g	1.1g
SODIUM	0.6g	0.4g
per FLAN	351 CAL	22.3g FAT
GUIDELINE DAILY AMOUNTS		
EACH DAY	WOMEN	MEN
Calories	2000	2500
Fat	70g	95g
OFFICIAL GOVERNMENT FIGURES FOR AVERAGE ADULTS		

• The **blue bar** at the base of the nutrition label shows you how many calories and how much fat is in a serving.

• The **Guideline Daily Amounts (GDA's)** can help you decide whether a product fits into your diet. They provide a guideline to the amount of fat and calories that you should have as part of a healthy diet. We have added GDA's to as many labels as possible.

helping you plan what you eat for a **healthier** vegetarian diet

Fruit and vegetables

• Aim to eat at least five portions of fruit and vegetables a day. Fresh, frozen, canned, dried and juiced varieties all count.

• Fruit and vegetables provide many vitamins and minerals needed for good health, as well as fibre which keeps the digestive system healthy.

The general healthy eating advice given to the general population also applies to vegetarians. A healthy diet includes plenty of fruit and vegetables and starchy foods, moderate amounts of alternatives to meat and fish, and moderate amounts of dairy products, and small amounts of foods containing fat and sugar.

Alternatives to meat and fish

• Eat some of these foods everyday to ensure an adequate intake of protein, vitamins and minerals.

• Eat a variety of these foods to ensure the right balance of proteins.

Text B

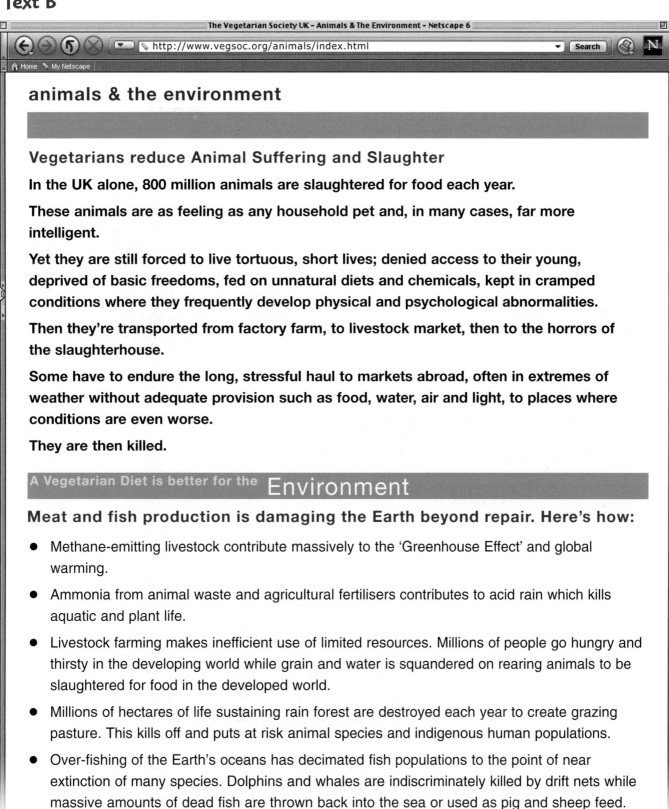

http://www.vegsoc.org/animals/index.html

Home   My Netscape

animals & the environment

Vegetarians reduce Animal Suffering and Slaughter

In the UK alone, 800 million animals are slaughtered for food each year.

These animals are as feeling as any household pet and, in many cases, far more intelligent.

Yet they are still forced to live tortuous, short lives; denied access to their young, deprived of basic freedoms, fed on unnatural diets and chemicals, kept in cramped conditions where they frequently develop physical and psychological abnormalities.

Then they're transported from factory farm, to livestock market, then to the horrors of the slaughterhouse.

Some have to endure the long, stressful haul to markets abroad, often in extremes of weather without adequate provision such as food, water, air and light, to places where conditions are even worse.

They are then killed.

A Vegetarian Diet is better for the Environment

Meat and fish production is damaging the Earth beyond repair. Here's how:

- Methane-emitting livestock contribute massively to the 'Greenhouse Effect' and global warming.

- Ammonia from animal waste and agricultural fertilisers contributes to acid rain which kills aquatic and plant life.

- Livestock farming makes inefficient use of limited resources. Millions of people go hungry and thirsty in the developing world while grain and water is squandered on rearing animals to be slaughtered for food in the developed world.

- Millions of hectares of life sustaining rain forest are destroyed each year to create grazing pasture. This kills off and puts at risk animal species and indigenous human populations.

- Over-fishing of the Earth's oceans has decimated fish populations to the point of near extinction of many species. Dolphins and whales are indiscriminately killed by drift nets while massive amounts of dead fish are thrown back into the sea or used as pig and sheep feed.

- Intensive grazing causes soil erosion and nutrient depletion.

These are just some of the many ways meat and fish production are harming our word. A vegetarian diet makes better use of the world's resources and is a highly effective way of positively contributing to our planet's future.

Together we can make the world a better place.

More articles about Animals and the Environment in The Vegetarian, which is published by The Vegetarian Society and is sent free of charge to all members.

Document: Done

Business ▲ Tech ▲ Fun ▲ Interact ▲

UNDERSTANDING THE TEXT

Start by looking at the two texts separately.

Text A: Leaflet

1 Write down three facts that are included in the text.

2 Look at the first sentence. Are the 7 million people mentioned all vegetarians?

3 What three reasons are given for people choosing a vegetarian lifestyle?

4 The leaflet gives information about different types of vegetarians. Which is the newest category?

5 How many Sainsbury's products carry the 'Healthy Balance' symbol?

Text B: Website

6 Write down three facts that are included in the text.

7 What reasons does this text suggest for being a vegetarian?

8 How does meat production damage rain forests?

INTERPRETING THE TEXT

9 Look at the three images in text A. What are they supposed to show the reader? Describe what each image shows. Then write a sentence saying why you think it has been chosen and how it helps persuade readers to think about becoming vegetarian.

Describe the image	Explain why you think it has been chosen

10 Look at the image in text B. Write a sentence about why it has been selected. How would this image help persuade a reader to think about becoming a vegetarian?

11 Look at text A. Is the text purely an information leaflet, or is it also an advertisement for Sainsbury's? How can you tell?

HINTS
- Look for any references to Sainsbury's in the text
- How is the supermarket being presented – what is its image?

12 Who do you think the two texts may be aimed at?

a vegetarians

b people thinking of becoming vegetarians

c meat eaters

d people interested in food and health

e older people

f younger people

Choose the *two* groups from the list above that you think are most suitable for each text, and write a sentence explaining why. Structure your answer like this:

Text A	Text B
The two definitions which best describe the target audience are ▲ ▲	The two definitions which best describe the target audience are ▲ ▲
… because …	… because …

LANGUAGE AND STRUCTURE

1 In information texts we often expect statements. Persuasive texts usually use more commands, where the verb is at the start ('*Eat* some of these foods each day').

In text A find:

a one statement

b one command.

2 We expect information texts to use factual language. This might include technical terms. Look at these technical terms and re-read the passage in text A where they are used. Write down what you think the highlighted part of each word might mean:

a **lacto**-vegetarians

b lacto-**ovo** vegetarians

c **demi**-vegetarians

3 Persuasive texts often use **emotive** words. These are words intended to get an emotional response from readers. Examples in text B are:

They're transported ... to the horrors of the slaughterhouse
Dolphins and whales are indiscriminately killed

a Think of some more neutral words which could have been used in these two examples.

b What is the effect of replacing the emotive words with more neutral ones?

4 In narrative texts, the paragraphs usually have to go in a certain order to make sense. In persuasive information texts, there is a less obvious story to tell. Look at the organization of the first six paragraphs in text B.

a For each of paragraphs 2-6 write down the word or phrase which is used to link it to the paragraph before. You should look for examples of:

Pronouns: *it / they / these / them*
Connectives: *despite this / then / yet / even / next / so*

b Would it be possible for these paragraphs to be organized in a different order? Could the text still make sense? Explain why or why not.

WRITING ACTIVITY

Using the information from the two texts, put together a poster giving arguments in favour of becoming a vegetarian. Aim to find eight reasons. Place them in order of most important reason (number 1) to least important reason (number 8). Think about how you will present the information and how you will use language, as well as images, to persuade your readers that they should seriously consider becoming vegetarians.

Extended Writing

Imagine that Sainsbury's want to use some of the information from text B in a future leaflet about vegetarian eating. The leaflet will be aimed at a young audience aged 11-14. They do not wish to use language that is too emotive, because it might upset some people, and also they do not want to put off customers who are happy eating meat.

Take some of the information from text B, and write it as it might appear in the Sainsbury's leaflet for children. Use this title, and then write a one-side leaflet:

Why you might want to cut down on eating meat

Think about:

◆ how you will present your leaflet – what images and design features you might use

◆ which arguments you might use to persuade readers to cut down their meat content

◆ how you will use language that is appropriate to an audience aged 11-14 – making it clear and informative, without seeming to talk down to them

◆ how you will reword some of the information from text B.

Speaking and listening
Special assignment

OBJECTIVES

This special assignment gives you the opportunity to hold a debate on a controversial topic. These are the objectives you will be studying:

- Speaking: *evaluate own talk*, and *standard English* (using this to justify an idea)

- Listening: *compare points of view, analyse bias*, and *identify issues*

- Group discussion: *evaluate own contributions*, (arriving at a) *considered viewpoint*, and (contributing to) *group organization*

A Initial brief

A group of students at your school has made this proposal to the headteacher:

Based on reliable research, we know that eating too much meat is bad for people. We also know that it involves cruelty to animals and it damages the environment. We therefore recommend that the school canteen should serve meat on only two out of every five days.

You are asked to make a group presentation either supporting this proposal or arguing against it. Your presentation should last five minutes, and will be followed by questions.

Work in a group of 3-5. Your teacher will ask you to take up a position – either in favour of or against the proposal. You will have one lesson in which to prepare your presentation.

B Research

1   In your group, brainstorm the arguments you will use to make your case. Use the two texts from Sainsbury's and the Vegetarian Society which you read on pages 113-116. You might also want to do additional research.

2 Make a list of the arguments your opponents will use. Think about how you could counter them.

3 Begin to structure your arguments into a presentation. Who will say what? What different roles will each of you take? Who will introduce your group, and the topic? Who will develop it? Who will conclude?

4 Think about questions you may be asked. Who will respond to them, and how?

5 Plan the format of the presentation in your group. How will you make the topic lively and entertaining, but not trivialize it? Will you use any visual aids? How will you make sure you can speak while making eye-contact with the audience, and don't rely too much on notes?

C Practice

Have a practice run-through of your presentation in your group. Give each other feedback on:

- how clearly you spoke
- whether the pace was right
- the way you engaged with the audience (eye contact, body language)
- whether your information and argument were clearly expressed.

D Presentation

Make your presentations. Ask questions after each one.

Afterwards, take a vote as to which team gave the best presentation – don't be influenced here by your own beliefs on vegetarianism.

Evaluate the debate.

- How could the presentations have been improved?
- Which persuasive techniques worked best?
- How could arguments have been better presented?
- How could the event have been better organized?
- What have you learnt about your own communication skills?

How explanation texts work

13

Introduction

We have looked at some explanation texts already in this book:

- Mobile Phones (page 24)
- Why is the Sky Blue? (page 80)

Explanation texts aim to explain how things work, why things happen, and to give us answers to questions.

They are usually clear and direct, and often begin with a general **opening statement**, then give a **step-by-step** account of an event or process. They often end with a **summary**.

Explanations usually use the **third person** and the **present tense**, but for writing about past events (historical writing) they will use the **past tense**.

Connectives are used to show how one idea relates to another and to indicate cause and effect.

Very precise terms, and sometimes **technical language**, are used in explanation texts, depending on how much the reader is likely to know about the topic.

Explanation texts emphasize **facts and causes**, and do not use much descriptive language.

Explaining a scientific report
Tollund Man

OBJECTIVES

This extract explains the results of a scientific investigation. These are the objectives you will be studying:

- Word level: *connectives for developing thought*
- Sentence level: *degrees of formality, paragraph organization*, and *sustained standard English*
- Reading: *information retrieval*
- Writing: *review own writing, exploratory writing, formal essay, narrative techniques*, and *explain connections*

Introduction

This extract is a school worksheet used for history pupils. It focuses on Tollund Man – the body of a man discovered in a Danish bog on 8 May 1950. Lying on his side, shrivelled, eyes closed, the man from the Tollund Fen was uncovered 2000 years after his death.

The worksheet is designed to help history students understand more about the investigation into Tollund Man. When you have studied it, you have the chance to write about it in contrasting ways.

The Mystery of Tollund Man

An early Spring day – 8th May 1950. Evening was gathering over Tollund Fen in Biaeldskor Dale in Denmark. The evening stillness was broken now and again by the call of the snipe. Two men were cutting peat for the tile stove and the kitchen range. As they worked they suddenly saw in the peat layer a face so fresh that they could only suppose that they had stumbled on a recent murder. They notified the police at Silkeborg, who came at once to the site. Bit by bit they began to remove the peat from the man's body till more of him became visible. The man lay on his right side just as if he was asleep. He lay 50 metres out from firm ground and had been covered by about 2 metres of peat, now dug away. On his head he wore a pointed skin cap fastened securely under the chin by a hide thong. Round his waist there was a smooth hide belt. Otherwise he was naked. His hair was cropped so short as to be almost entirely hidden by his cap. He was clean-shaven but there was very short stubble on the chin and upper lip.

The air of gentle peace about the man was shattered when a small lump of peat was removed from beside his head. Underneath was a rope, made of two leather thongs twisted together. This was a noose. It was drawn tight around his neck and throat and then coiled like a snake over his shoulder and down across his back.

Who was this man? How long had he lain there beneath the earth? What was the cause of his death?

Scientific report on the body

The body was removed from the bog and examined by doctors and scientists. They came to the following conclusions:

1 Date of burial

Underneath the body was a thin layer of moss. Scientists know that this was formed in Danish peat bogs in the early Iron Age, about the time when Christ was born. The body must, therefore, have been put in a hole in the peat roughly *2000* years ago in the Early Iron Age. The acid in the peat had prevented the body decaying – it looked as if it had been recently buried.

2 Cause of death

Examinations and X-rays showed that the man's head was undamaged, and his heart, lungs and liver were also well preserved. He was not an old man though he must have been over 20 years old because his wisdom teeth had grown. He had therefore probably been killed by the rope round his neck. This noose had left clear marks on the skin under the chin and at the sides of his neck but there was no mark at the back of the neck where the knot was. It was impossible to tell if his neck had been broken because the bones were very crumbly.

3 His last meal

The stomach and intestines were examined and tests were carried out on their contents. The scientists discovered that the man's last meal had been a kind of soup made from vegetables and seeds, some cultivated and some wild, such as barley, linseed, 'gold of pleasure', knot-weed, bristlegrass and camomile.

There were no traces of meat and from the stage of digestion it was obvious that the man had lived for 12-24 hours after this meal. In other words he had not eaten for a day before his death. Although such a vegetable soup was not unusual for people of this time, two interesting things were noted:

a) the soup contained many different kinds of wild and cultivated seeds and some of them must have been gathered deliberately, because they were not always easy to find. The soup was, therefore, probably for a special occasion.

b) the soup was made up from seeds which were connected *only with the spring*.

UNDERSTANDING THE TEXT

1 How did scientists work out that the man must have been put in the bog around 2000 years earlier?

2 How old was he?

3 How could scientists tell his age?

4 What is known about the way he died?

5 What clue was there that a special occasion had taken place?

INTERPRETING THE TEXT

6 What can you deduce from the man's last meal about the community he lived in and their habits?

7 What mysteries are there surrounding the death of Tollund Man?

8 The text contains many factual details.

    a Write down one fact.

    b Does it contain any personal opinions? If so, write them down; if not, explain why not.

LANGUAGE AND STRUCTURE

1 Like most explanatory texts, this one is written in the third-person form. It never uses the pronouns 'I' or 'me'.

    a Why do you think this is?

    b Would the worksheet be less or more interesting to read if it used a more personal style?

2 Look at the first sentence under the heading 'Scientific report on the body'. It uses the passive voice ('The body was removed … by …').

    a How could the writer have written this sentence using the active voice?

    b Why do you think the passive voice has been used?

3 The worksheet is aimed at students aged about 14. What clues are there in the language that this is the writer's target audience, rather than doctors and scientists?

You might comment on:

- the length and types of sentences
- the structure of the explanation
- the use of vocabulary.

4 Look at the structure of the worksheet:

- general introduction
- three subheadings with explanations beneath each one.

Could the subheadings ('Date of Burial, Cause of Death, His Last Meal') have been placed in any order, or did it need to be this particular order?

5 Choose two sentences whose meaning is linked, and show how the writer links the ideas in the second sentence back to the ideas in the first. What are the linking words or phrases?

WRITING ACTIVITY

Two different types of writing assignment could be set for pupils reading this handout. A history teacher could set an essay about the facts; an English teacher could ask for an imaginative account of what Tollund Man might be thinking and feeling.

Write the opening paragraphs of these two assignments.

Assignments:

History	English
Write a factual report about Tollund Man – who he was, what we know about his society, and how he might have been killed.	Imagine you are Tollund Man. You have been dug up after 2000 years at rest, and scientists are prodding at your body. What thoughts are going through your mind?
Sample starter: Tollund Man was dug from a Danish peat bog dating from …	Sample starter: Light again – it's years since I last saw light …

Write a brief paragraph explaining how you approached the two tasks, and how you chose a style that was appropriate for each.

How successful did you feel each of your openings was in fulfilling its purpose? Were you more skilled at writing in one style than the other?

Unit 13 EXTENDED WRITING

Use this activity to help you review an essay you have recently written in English or another subject.

A checklist is given below to help you evaluate how well you have written the work. Aim to write four brief paragraphs about the essay, one under each heading.

A Structure

* How have you structured the assignment?

* Why did you structure it in this way?

* Have you given a general statement near the beginning (if appropriate) and then explored different examples?

* Have you used quotations or specific examples to support your ideas?

* Have you shaped your writing into coherent paragraphs?

* Have you used connectives like *another, although, however* to link ideas together?

* How could you have improved the structure?

B Sentences

* What types of sentences have you used – is there a variety of short and long sentences? Have you used only statements, or commands and questions also?

* Have you kept the style factual, rather than descriptive?

* Have you kept the tone impersonal, rather than using 'I' and 'me' too much?

* How could you have improved your use of sentences?

C Words

- How have you used your vocabulary – have you chosen words that are appropriate for the topic?

- Have you used formal vocabulary, and technical words when necessary?

- Have you avoided contractions such as 'isn't' or 'weren't', to create a more formal tone?

- How might you have improved your use of vocabulary?

D Overall evaluation

Write a final sentence or two, saying how effective you feel your assignment is. Be as clear as you can about its strengths and weaknesses.

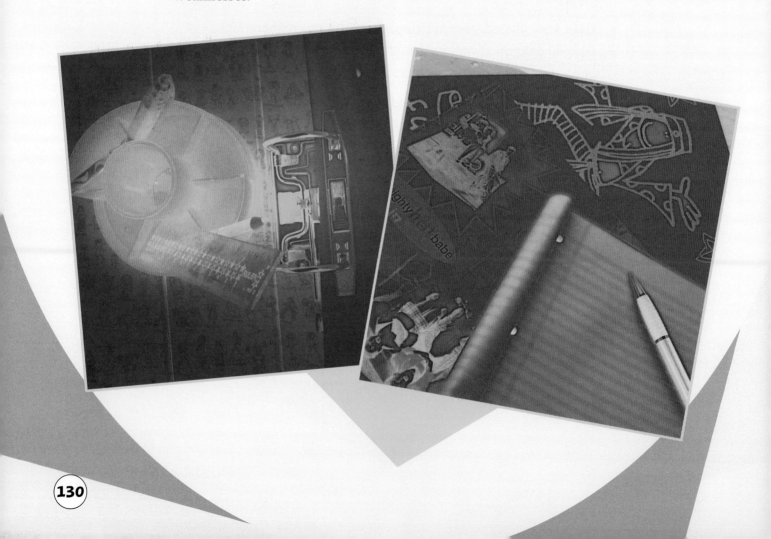

Parody

Introduction

Once you become familiar with the way different non-fiction texts are written, it can be entertaining to play around with the conventions and rules.

A lot of comedy shows and films do this kind of thing. For example, the 'Airplane' movies took the conventions of disaster films and made them funny; comedy programmes like 'The Fast Show' imitate news or documentary programmes.

Poking fun at a style of text or programme in this creative way is known as **parody**. This unit looks at one specific example of a parody – the way the magazine *Private Eye* uses the conventions of a newspaper to retell some parts of the story of *Macbeth*.

Parodies often use the conventions of a well-known type of text (e.g. news bulletins, documentaries, newspaper reports) and apply them to unexpected subject matter.

Parody of a newspaper report
The Glamis Herald

> ### OBJECTIVES
>
> This extract takes the events of a Shakespeare play and creates a parody of a newspaper report about politicians. You will be studying these objectives:
>
> - Word level: *layers of meaning*
> - Sentence level: *exploit conventions*
> - Reading: *readers and texts* (how they influence each other), and *author's standpoint*
> - Writing: *'infotainment'* (how information texts can be amusing and entertaining), and *descriptive detail*

Introduction

Private Eye is a satirical magazine. This means that it pokes fun at the government, politicians and celebrities. Sometimes the tone of this is humorous and playful (parody); sometimes it is much more critical (satire). When you have studied this text, you will have a chance to write a parody of your own.

This article uses the conventions of a daily newspaper to present the story of *Macbeth* ... which has itself been updated to hint at the former President of the USA, Bill Clinton, and his wife Hillary.

To understand the way the parody works it would be most helpful to know something about Shakespeare's play *Macbeth*. If you have not studied it, you can read a summary of the play on page 137.

> ### GLOSSARY
> **thane** – *knight or duke*

The Glamis Herald

Macbeth defends wife – 'Saintly, selfless public servant' says former Thane

By HENRY THE PORTER

The controversial new king of Scotland, King Macbeth, today spoke out in defence of his wife, Lady Hillary Macbeth, whom many critics have called 'the power behind the throne'.

Cawdor What A Scorcher

At an emotional press conference in the dungeon of the Castle, the king told scribes of his deep distress over the recent 'Duncangate' allegations.

- **It is rumoured that the unexpected death of King Duncan, a close member of the Macbeth circle, may well have had something to do with the Macbeths and Lady Macbeth in particular.**

- **It is further claimed that the suicide of long-term Macbeth associate, Banquo, may also have had a political motive.**

But the king firmly rebutted any such reports, saying: 'My wife has the finest moral compass of anyone I know.' He also said that the allegations had left Lady Macbeth very distressed and that she had to call in medical help following attacks of sleepwalking.

Banker's Ghost

There were also unconfirmed reports that the King himself had been subject to hallucinations and that a recent reception at the castle had to be called off suddenly after the king was 'taken ill'. Suggestions that the king may have 'seen ghosts' were dismissed by an official spokesman.

Weather Forecast for Tomorrow and Tomorrow and Tomorrow
With IAN MACBETHKILL

A LARGE area of trees is now on the move in the Birnam area which is expected to reach Dunsinane by tomorrow midday.

Cooking Tips
With THE WEIRD SISTERS

TAKE ONE Eye of Newt, one Toe of Frog, one Wool of Bat and one Tongue of Dog. Bring to the boil and put in the microwave in a non-metallic receptacle.
(Shurely shome mishtake?)

On Other Pages

UNDERSTANDING THE TEXT

1 Write down two features which make the text look like a real newspaper.

2 What is the gist of the 'story' that the text is reporting?

3 Who is Banquo, according to the article?

4 Why is Hillary Macbeth upset?

INTERPRETING THE TEXT

5 The text makes a lot of jokey references to *Macbeth*. Imagine the newspaper is being read by someone who does not know Shakespeare's play. Choose one of the examples below and explain the joke:

   a The recent 'Duncangate' allegations

   b Weather Forecast for Tomorrow and Tomorrow and Tomorrow

   c Cooking Tips with the Weird Sisters

6 The text also makes reference to ex-President Clinton and his wife. What does the author's style suggest about his attitude towards them?

7 These are some of the features we expect in newspapers. For each one, write down an example from this text.

Feature	Example
Headline to grab the reader's attention	
Byline (telling us the name of the writer)	
Subheadings to break up the text	
A topic sentence which tells the whole story at the start of the article	
Trails for other features in the newspaper	
Advertising	

8 Write a short paragraph about your response to the text.

    a What do you like about it? Which jokes do you find funny? Which bits do not make sense? How could it be funnier?

    b What does it suggest to you about the writer's attitude to powerful politicians, and the way they are usually presented in newspaper reports?

LANGUAGE AND STRUCTURE

1 Newspaper headlines often have certain key features. Look at the features below and write down an example from this text.

    a They use the present tense.

    b They use alliteration (repetition of initial consonants).

    c They are telegrammatic – they miss out grammatical words like *the/his/their*.

2 The sentence style in newspapers often uses a lot of modification. This means giving as much detail as possible in each sentence. Take this sentence:

An English teacher today bought a new car.

Reported in a newspaper, this might begin:

Trendy English teacher Jez Foley, 24, yesterday amazed pupils at Long Melford High School …

Notice how the writer uses labels ('trendy', '24') to add details to the subject of the sentence.

Now look at the first sentence of the *Glamis Herald*. How does the writer use a similar technique in writing about Macbeth?

3 Newspapers sometimes use the passive voice, like this:

Suggestions that the king may have 'seen ghosts' were dismissed by an official spokesman.

    a Write this sentence in the active voice.

    b Why do you think newspapers sometimes use the passive voice in this way?

4 Some of the writing in the text is funny because of its reference to *Macbeth* or the Clintons. Some is funny because it uses wordplay or puns.

Choose one example from those below and explain how the writer is playing with words:

a Cawdor What a Scorcher

b Angus McDeayton

c Ian Macbethkill.

WRITING ACTIVITY

Write your own headline and topic sentence for a spoof newspaper article using one of these examples:

◆ the Shakespeare play you are reading

◆ another text you have recently read

◆ a fairy story or legend.

Look back at your answers to the questions above to remind yourself of the key features of headlines and newspaper style.

Summary of *Macbeth* by William Shakespeare

Macbeth wins honour in battle for Scotland. Afterwards, Macbeth and his fellow officer Banquo meet some witches stirring their cauldron on the battlefield. They prophesy that Macbeth will gain a new title, and that later he will become king of Scotland. When Macbeth and Banquo present themselves to King Duncan, he decides to reward Macbeth with the title Thane of Cawdor, but he declares his own son, Malcolm, to be the heir to the kingdom.

King Duncan then visits Macbeth's castle. Macbeth is driven on by his wife to kill the king that night. When the king is found stabbed, Banquo and another lord, Macduff, begin to suspect Macbeth.

Macbeth becomes king. He then arranges the murder of Banquo, without Lady Macbeth's knowledge. At a ceremonial banquet that night, Banquo's ghost appears to Macbeth and the meal is disrupted. Macbeth meets up with the witches again, who tell him of further prophecies. He feels sure that he can get rid of all possible enemies and remain as king.

Macbeth sends attackers to Macduff's castle, and Lady Macduff and her children are killed. Macduff himself has already escaped and he becomes Malcolm's ally. Lady Macbeth dies, deranged by guilt and grief, and Malcolm's troops advance towards Macbeth's besieged castle. All the witches' prophecies are shown to be tricks, and Macbeth is killed in the battle - his head is brought to Malcolm by Macduff. Order is restored for Scotland, and Malcolm becomes king.

EXTENDED WRITING

Choose a non-fiction genre and write a parody of a text you know well. For example, you could choose:

◆ a news report on the feud between the Capulets and the Montagues, including on-the-spot interviews with the fathers of Romeo and Juliet

◆ an encyclopaedia entry for the Hogwarts School, or another famous location from a book you have read

◆ a page from an instruction book on how to care for angels (based on *Skellig*).

Other possible text-types:

◆ an extract from a school textbook

◆ a report of an event or experiment

◆ sports journalism or commentary

◆ a speech

◆ a newspaper editorial.

Hints

● To make it entertaining, match your text type with an unusual topic, such as one of those listed above.

● To make it funny, treat the topic seriously (e.g. write your instructions on caring for angels as if they are deadly serious). Include vivid details to bring your topic to life.

● Remind yourself of the language features of the text type you are using by looking back at the introduction pages for text types in this book.

● Do not aim to write too much – the focus should be on the quality of your parody, not the amount you write.